The Beatles Logo is a trademark of Apple Corps Ltd.

ISBN 0-634-02557-0

HAL•LEONARD®
CORPORATION
7777 W. BLUEMOUND RD. P.O. BOX 13819 MILWAUKEE, WI 53213

Visit Hal Leonard Online at
www.halleonard.com

CONTENTS

STRUM AND PICK PATTERNS

This chart contains the suggested strum and pick patterns that are referred to by number at the beginning of each song in this book. The symbols ⊓ and ⌄ in the strum patterns refer to down and up strokes, respectively. The letters in the pick patterns indicate which right-hand fingers plays which strings.

p = thumb
i = index finger
m = middle finger
a = ring finger

For example; Pick Pattern 2
is played: thumb - index - middle - ring

Strum Patterns

Pick Patterns

You can use the 3/4 Strum or Pick Patterns in songs written in compound meter (6/8, 9/8, 12/8, etc.).
For example, you can accompany a song in 6/8 by playing the 3/4 pattern twice in each measure.
The 4/4 Strum and Pick Patterns can be used for songs written in cut time (¢) by doubling the note time values in the patterns. Each pattern would therefore last two measures in cut time.

And I Love Her

Words and Music by John Lennon and Paul McCartney

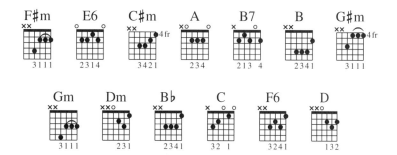

Intro
Moderately

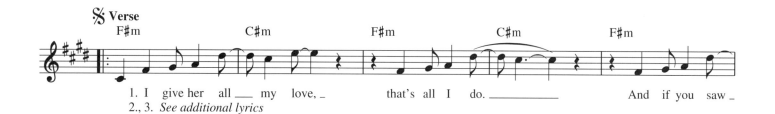

1. I give her all __ my love, _ that's all I do. _____ And if you saw _
2., 3. *See additional lyrics*

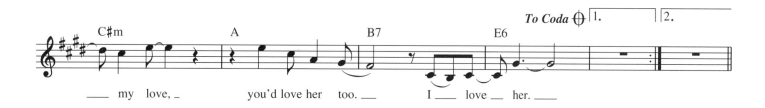

__ my love, _ you'd love her too. __ I __ love __ her. __

Bridge

A love like ours __ could nev-er die __ as long as I __

__ have you near _ me. __

Verse

4. Bright are the stars ___ that shine, ___ dark is the sky. ___ I know this

love of mine ___ will nev-er die. ___ And I love ___ her. ___

Outro

Additional Lyrics

2. She gives me ev'rything, and tenderly.
   The kiss my lover brings she brings to me.
   And I love her.

3. Bright are the stars that shine, dark is the sky.
   I know this love of mine will never die.
   And I love her.

Baby You're a Rich Man

Words and Music by John Lennon and Paul McCartney

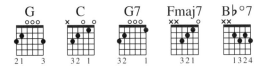

Strum Pattern: 2
Pick Pattern: 4

Verse
Moderately

1. How does it feel ___ to be one of the beau - ti - ful peo - ple?

Now that you know ___ who you are, ___ what do you want ___ to be? ___

And have you trav - elled ver - y far, ___ far as the eye ___ can see? ___

Verse

2., 3. How does it feel ___ to be - one of the beau - ti ful peo - ple?

How of - ten have ___ you been there, ___ of - ten e - nough ___ to know? ___
Tuned to a nat - ur - al E _____ hap - py to be _____ that way. ___

What did you see ___ when you were there, ___ no - thing that does - n't show? ___
Now that you've found ___ an - oth - er key, ___ what are you go'n' ___ to play? ___

Chorus

Ba - by you're a rich man. Ba - by you're a rich man. Ba - by you're a rich man

too. ___ You keep all your mon - ey in a big brown bag ___ in side - a zoo, ___

___ what a thing to do. _____ Ba - by you're a rich man.

Ba - by you're a rich man. Ba - by you're a rich man too. ___

Outro-Chorus

Repeat and fade

Ba - by you're a rich man. Ba - by you're a rich man. Ba - by you're a rich man too. ___

Across the Universe

Words and Music by John Lennon and Paul McCartney

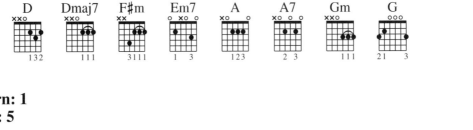

*Strum Pattern: 1
*Pick Pattern: 5

Verse
Slowly

1. Words are flow-ing out ___ like end - less rain ___ in - to a pa - per cup, ___ they

*Combine Patterns 9 & 10 for $\frac{5}{4}$ meas.
Use Pattern 10 for $\frac{2}{4}$ meas.

slith - er while _ they pass, they slip a - way ___ a - cross the u - ni - verse. ___ Pools of sor - row, waves of joy are

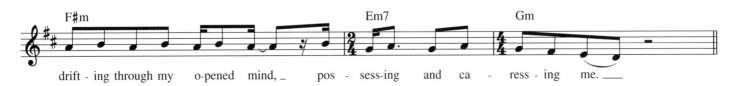

drift - ing through my o - pened mind, _ pos - sess - ing and ca - ress - ing me. ___

𝄋 Chorus

Jai ___ Gu - ru ___ De - va. ___ Om. ___

Noth - ing's gon - na change my world. _ Noth - ing's gon - na change my world. _

To Coda ⊕

Noth - ing's gon - na change my world. _ Noth - ing's gon - na change my world. _

Verse

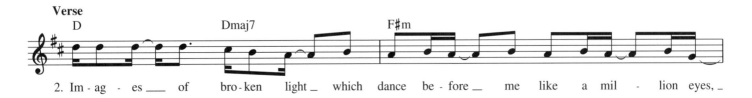

2. Im - ag - es ___ of bro - ken light _ which dance be - fore _ me like a mil - lion eyes, _

_____ they call me on and on _ a-cross _ the u - ni - verse. _ Thoughts me-an - der like a rest - less

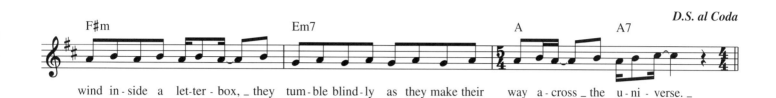

D.S. al Coda

wind in - side a let-ter - box, _ they tum-ble blind-ly as they make their way a-cross _ the u - ni - verse. _

✛ Coda
Verse

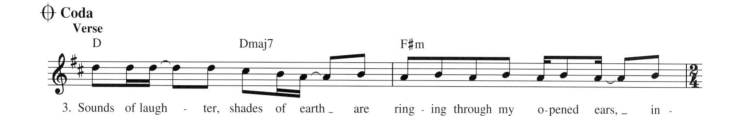

3. Sounds of laugh - ter, shades of earth _ are ring - ing through my o-pened ears, _ in -

cit - ing and in - vit - ing me. ___ Lim - it - less, _ un - dy - ing love, _ which

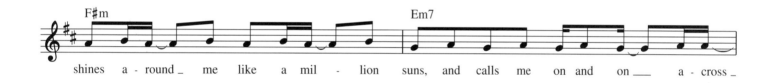

shines a - round _ me like a mil - lion suns, and calls me on and on ___ a - cross _

Chorus

____ the u - ni - verse. _ Jai __ Gu - ru _____ De - va. __ Om. ____

Noth - ing's gon - na change my world. __ Noth - ing's gon - na change my world. _

Outro   *Repeat and fade*

____ Jai ____ Gu - ru _____ De - va. ____

Act Naturally

Words and Music by Vonie Morrison and Johnny Russell

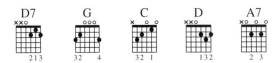

Strum Pattern: 3
Pick Pattern: 5

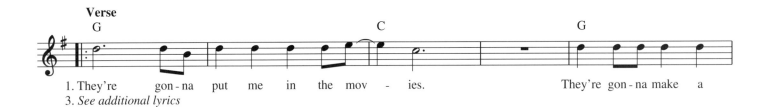

1. They're gon-na put me in the mov-ies. They're gon-na make a
3. *See additional lyrics*

big star out of me. We'll make a film __ a-bout a man that's sad and lone-

-ly, and all I got-ta do is act nat-'ral-ly.

Well, I bet you I'm gon-na be a big __ star. Might

win an "Os-car", you can __ nev-er tell. __ The mov-ies gon-na

make   me   a   big ___ star   'cause   I   can   play   the   part   so

well.   2., 4. Well,   I   hope   you   come   and   see   me   in   the   mov - ies.

Then I'll   know   that   you ___   will   plain - ly   see   the

big - gest   fool   that   ev - er   hit   the   big - time,   and

all   I   got - ta   do   is   act   nat - 'ral - ly.

Outro

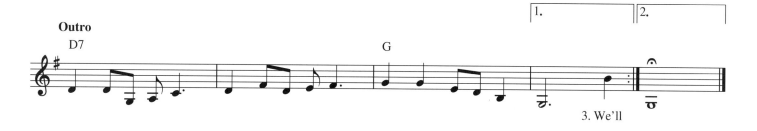

3. We'll

Additional Lyrics

3. We'll make the scene about a man that's sad and lonely,
   And beggin' down upon his bended knee.
   I'll play the part but I won't need rehearsin'.
   All I have to do is act nat'rally.

All My Loving

Words and Music by John Lennon and Paul McCartney

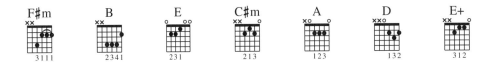

Strum Pattern: 3, 4
Pick Pattern: 1, 4

𝄋 **Verse**

Brightly

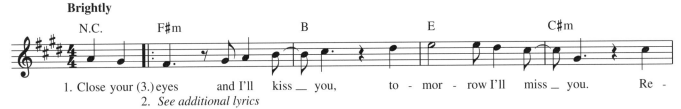

1. Close your (3.) eyes and I'll kiss __ you, to - mor - row I'll miss __ you. Re -
2. *See additional lyrics*

mem - ber __ I'll al - ways be true. And then

while I'm a - way, __ I'll write home ev - 'ry day. __ And I'll

send all my lov - ing to you. __ 2. I'll pre -

All my lov - ing, __ I __ will send to

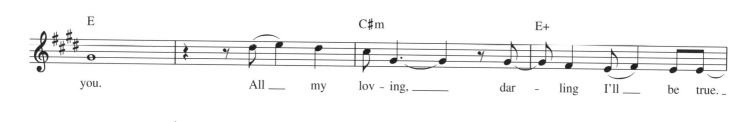

you. All __ my lov - ing, _____ dar - ling I'll __ be true. __

To Coda ⊕

Guitar Solo

D.S. al Coda
(take 2nd ending)

3. Close your

⊕ **Coda**

Outro-Chorus

All __ my lov - ing, _____ all _____ my __

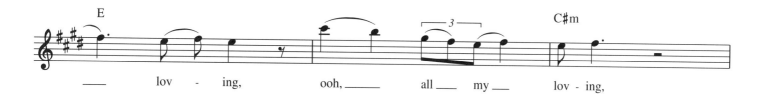

__ lov - ing, ooh, _____ all __ my __ lov - ing,

I will send __ to you.

Additional Lyrics

2. I'll pretend that I'm kissing
   The lips I am missing.
   And hope that my dreams will come true.
   And then while I'm away
   I'll write home ev'ryday.
   And I'll send all my loving to you.

All You Need Is Love

Words and Music by John Lennon and Paul McCartney

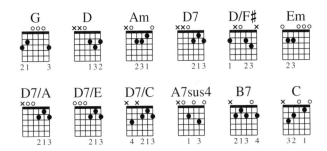

*Strum Pattern: 4
*Pick Pattern: 3

Intro-Chorus
Moderately

*Use Pattern 9 for $\frac{3}{4}$ meas., and Pattern 10 for $\frac{2}{4}$ meas.

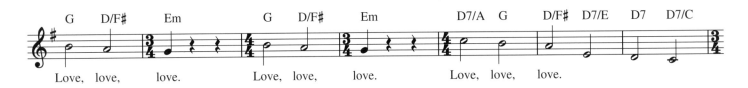

Love, love, love. Love, love, love. Love, love, love.

1. There's noth-ing you can do that can't be done. ___
2., 3. *See additional lyrics*

Noth-ing you can sing that can't be sung. ___ Noth-ing you can say but you can learn _

___ how to play the game. _ It's eas - y.

Chorus

All you need is love. ___ All you need is love. ___

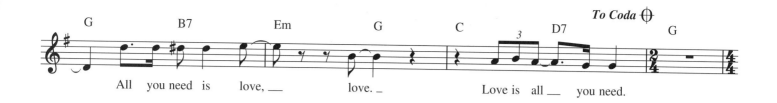

All you need is love, __ love. __ Love is all __ you need.

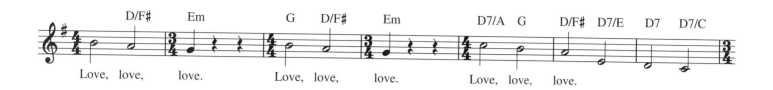

Love, love, love. Love, love, love. Love, love, love.

All you need is love. __ All you need is love. __

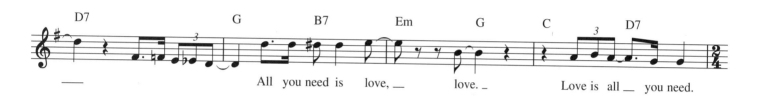

__ All you need is love, __ love. __ Love is all __ you need.

D.S. al Coda
(take 2nd ending)

Coda

Outro-Chorus

All you need is love. ___

__ *Spoken:* All to-geth-er now. __ All you need is love. _ *Spoken:* Ev-'ry-bod-y. All you need is love, _

Repeat and fade

__ love. _ Love is all __ you need. Love is all ___ you need. Love is all __

Additional Lyrics

2. There's nothing you can make that can't be made.
   No one you can save that can't be saved.
   Nothing you can do but you can learn how to be you in time.
   It's easy.

3. There's nothing you can know that isn't known.
   Nothing you can see that isn't shown.
   Nowhere you can be that isn't where you're meant to be.
   It's easy.

And Your Bird Can Sing

Words and Music by John Lennon and Paul McCartney

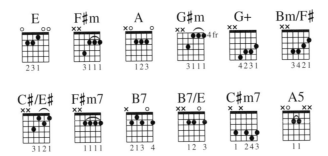

Strum Pattern: 5
Pick Pattern: 4

Intro

Moderate Rock

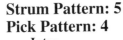

Verse

1. Tell me that you've got ev-'ry thing you want, and your bird can sing, but you don't get me, _
2. *See additional lyrics*

| 1. | 2. |

_ you don't get me.

𝄋 Bridge

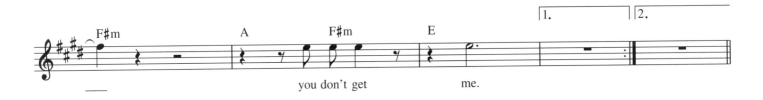

When your prized _ pos-ses - sions start to weigh _ you down, _
See additional lyrics

To Coda ⊕

look in my _ di - rec - tion, I'll be 'round, _ I'll be 'round. _

Interlude

D.S. al Coda

✛ **Coda**

Verse

3. You tell me that you've heard ev-'ry sound there is, and your bird can

swing, but you can't hear me, _____ you can't hear me.

Outro

Additional Lyrics

2. You say you've seen seven wonders,
   And your bird is green,
   But you can't see me,
   You can't see me.

Bridge When your bird is broken,
   Will it bring you down?
   You may be awoken,
   I'll be 'round, I'll be 'round.

Back in the U.S.S.R.

Words and Music by John Lennon and Paul McCartney

E7   A   D   C   E   Gadd9   D♭   B   D7

Strum Pattern: 1
Pick Pattern: 1

Intro
Moderately fast Rock

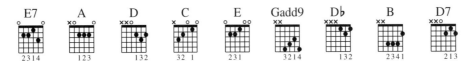

1. Flew in from Mi - a - mi Beach, B. O. A. C., ___ did -
2., 3. *See additional lyrics*

- n't get to bed last night. ___ On ___ the way the pa - per bag was

on my knee. ___ Man, ___ I had a dread - ful flight. ___ I'm back in the U. S. S. R., ___

___ you don't ___ know how luck - y you are, ___ boy. ___

Back in the U. S. S. R. ___   Back in the U. S.,

back in the U. S.,   back in the U. S. S. R. ___   Well, the

U - kraine girls real - ly knock me out, ___ they leave the ___ west be - hind. ___ And

Mos - cow girls make me sing and shout, _ that Geor - gia's al - ways on my mi - mi - mi - mi - mi - mi - mi - mi ___ mind. _

Additional Lyrics

2. Been away so long I hardly knew the place,
Gee, it's good to get back home.
Leave it 'til tomorrow to unpack my case,
Honey, disconnect the phone.

3. Show me 'round your snow-peaked mountains way down south,
Take me to your daddy's farm.
Let me hear your balalaikas ringing out,
Come and keep your comrade warm.

The Ballad of John and Yoko

Words and Music by John Lennon and Paul McCartney

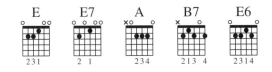

Strum Pattern: 1
Pick Pattern: 5

Verse
Moderate Rock

1. Stand-in' in the dock at South-amp - ton, try'n' to get to Hol-land or France. _
2. – 5. *See additional lyrics*

The man in the mac _ said, _ "You've got to go back." _ You know they

did - n't e - ven give us a chance. _ Christ! You know it ain't eas - y, _____

you know how hard it can be. ____ The way things are go - in'

5th time, To Coda

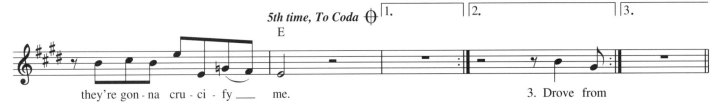

they're gon - na cru - ci - fy ___ me.   3. Drove from

Bridge

Sav-ing up your mon-ey for a rain - y day, _ giv-ing all your clothes to char - i - ty.

Last night the wife said, "Oh boy, when you're dead, you don't take noth - ing with you but your

D.C. al Coda
(take repeat)   Coda

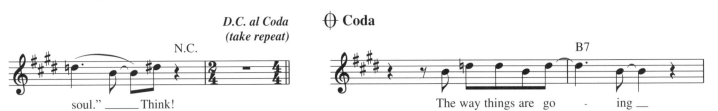

soul." _____Think!   The way things are go - ing ___

they're go'n' to cru - ci - fy _____ me.

Outro

Additional Lyrics

2. Finally made the plane into Paris,
Honeymoonin' down by the Seine.
Peter Brown called to say, "You can make it O.K.,
You can get married in Gibraltar near Spain."
Christ! You know it ain't easy.
You know how hard it can be.
The way things are goin'
They're gonna crucify me.

3. Drove from Paris to the Amsterdam Hilton,
Talkin' in our beds for a week.
The news people said, "Say, what're you doin' in bed?"
I said, "We're only try'n' to get us some peace."
Christ! You know it ain't easy.
You know how hard it can be.
The way things are goin'
They're gonna crucify me.

4. Made a lightnin' trip to Vienna,
Eating choc'late cake in a bag.
The newspapers said, "She's gone to his head;
They look just like two Gurus in drag."
Christ! You know it ain't easy.
You know how hard it can be.
The way things are goin'
They're gonna crucify me.

5. Caught an early plane back to London,
Fifty acorns tied in a sack.
The men from the press said, "We wish you success.
It's good to have the both of you back."
Christ! You know it ain't easy.
You know how hard it can be.
The way things are goin'
They're gonna crucify me.

Because

Words and Music by John Lennon and Paul McCartney

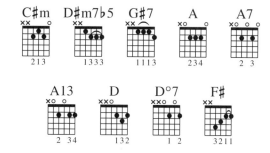

Strum Pattern: 1
Pick Pattern: 2

Intro

Moderately slow

Ah, _____ 1. Be -

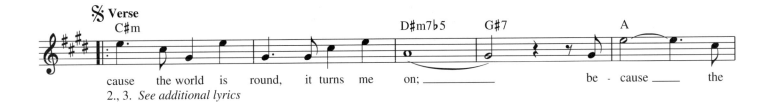

Verse

cause the world is round, it turns me on; _____ be - cause _____ the

2., 3. *See additional lyrics*

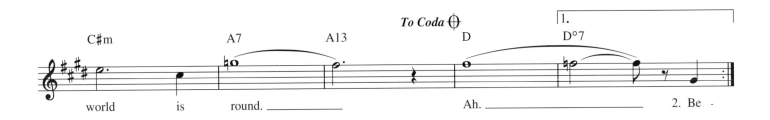

To Coda

world is round. _____ Ah. _____ 2. Be -

2.

Bridge   *D.S. al Coda*

_____ Love is old, love is new; love is all, love is you. 3. Be -

Coda   **Outro**

Ah. _____

Ah. _____

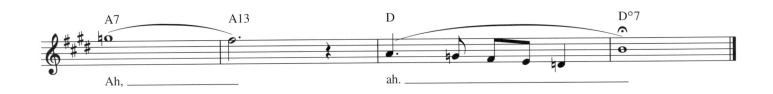

Ah, _____ ah. _____

Additional Lyrics

2. Because the wind is high, it blows my mind;
   Because the wind is high.
   Ah.

3. Because the sky is blue, it makes me cry;
   Because the sky is blue.
   Ah.

Blackbird

Words and Music by John Lennon and Paul McCartney

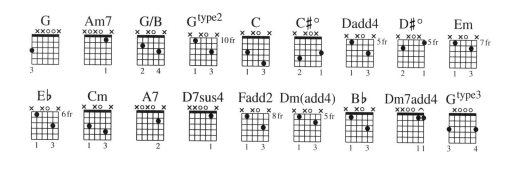

G   Am7   G/B   G^type2   C   C♯°   Dadd4   D♯°   Em

E♭   Cm   A7   D7sus4   Fadd2   Dm(add4)   B♭   Dm7add4   G^type3

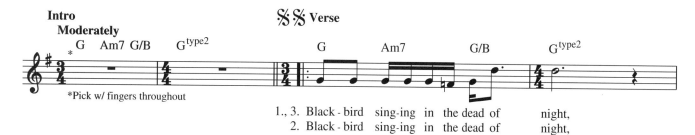

Intro
Moderately

*Pick w/ fingers throughout

𝄋 𝄋 **Verse**

1., 3. Black - bird sing-ing in the dead of night,
2. Black - bird sing-ing in the dead of night,

take _ these bro-ken wings _ and learn _ to fly. __
take _ these sunk-en eyes __ and learn _ to see. __ }

All your _ life, _

To Coda 2

__ you were on - ly wait - ing for the mo - ment to a - rise. _

2.

𝄋 **Bridge**

- ment to be _ free. Black - bird __ fly, ___ black - bird __ fly _

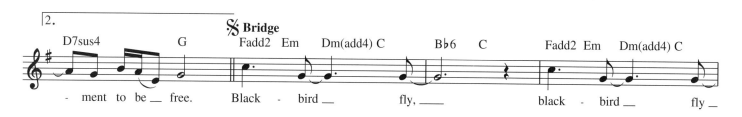

Interlude

To Coda 1

__ in - to the light ___ of the dark black _____ night. _

D.S. al Coda 1

23

⊕ **Coda 1**

— night.

⊕ **Coda 2**

you were on - ly wait-ing for this mo - ment to a - rise. —

You were on - ly — wait-ing for this mo - ment to a - rise. _____

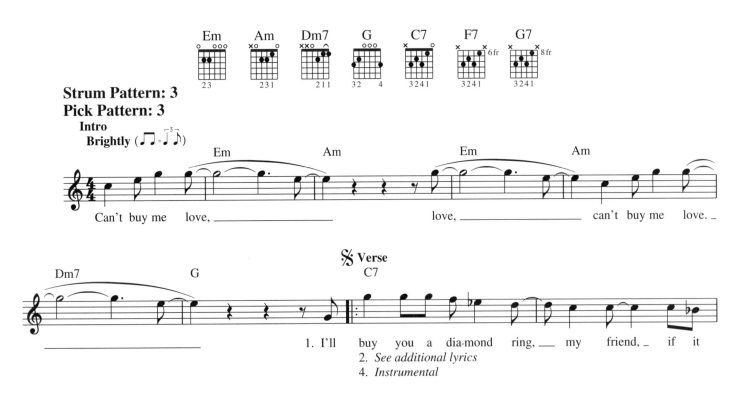

You were on - ly wait-ing — for this mo - ment to a - rise. —

Can't Buy Me Love

Words and Music by John Lennon and Paul McCartney

Strum Pattern: 3
Pick Pattern: 3

Intro
Brightly

Can't buy me love, _____ love, _____ can't buy me love. —

%̸ Verse

1. I'll buy you a dia-mond ring, — my friend, — if it
2. *See additional lyrics*
4. *Instrumental*

Additional Lyrics

2. I'll give you all I've got to give,
   If you say you love me too.
   I may not have a lot to give,
   But what I got I'll give to you.
   I don't care too much for money,
   For money can't buy me love.

Birthday

Words and Music by John Lennon and Paul McCartney

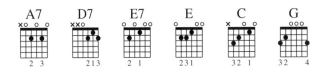

Strum Pattern: 6
Pick Pattern: 4

Intro
Moderately fast Rock

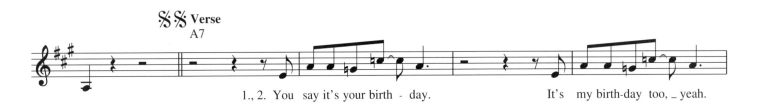

1., 2. You say it's your birth - day. It's my birth-day too, _ yeah.

They say it's your birth - day. We're gon-na have a good time. I'm

glad it's your birth - day, hap - py birth - day to ___ you.

Yes, we're go-in' to a par - ty, par - ty. Yes, we're go-in' to a par - ty, par - ty.

%S Chorus

Yes, we're go-in' to a par - ty, par - ty.   I would like you to dance, _

(Birth - day.) _ take a cha-cha-cha - chance, _   (Birth - day.) _ I would like you to dance, _

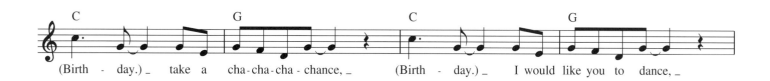

To Coda 1

(Birth - day.) _   dance! _____

Guitar Solo

D.S. al Coda 1   ⊕ **Coda 1**   ⊕ **Coda 2**

D.S.S. al Coda 2

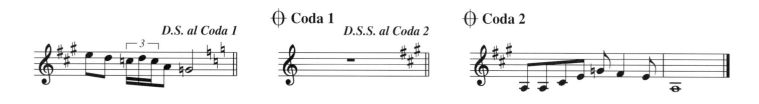

Come Together

Words and Music by John Lennon and Paul McCartney

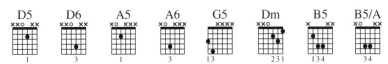

Strum Pattern: 1

Verse
Slow Rock

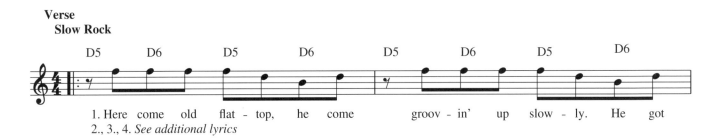

1. Here come old flat - top, he come groov - in' up slow - ly. He got
2., 3., 4. *See additional lyrics*

Joo Joo eye - ball, he one ho - ly roll - er. He got hair down

to his knee. ___ Got to be a jok - er, he just do what he please. ___

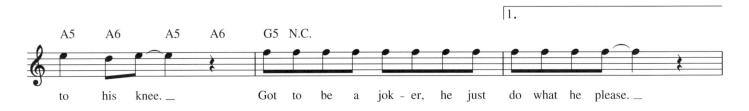

got to be free. Come to - geth - er right now, ___ o - ver

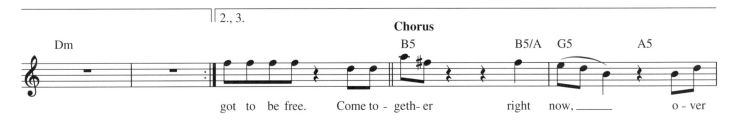

me.

4.

Chorus

so hard to see. ___ Come to - geth - er right now, ___ o - ver

Dm

me.

Outro

Repeat and fade

D5 D6 D5 D6 D5 D6 D5 D6 D5 D6 D5 D6 D5 D6 D5 D6

Come to-geth-er,   yeah.   Come to-geth-er,   yeah.

Additional Lyrics

2. He wear no shoeshine, he got
   Toe jam football. He got
   Monkey finger, he shoot
   Coca Cola. He say,
   "I know you, you know me."
   One thing I can tell you is you got to be free.

3. He bag production, he got
   Walrus gumboot. He got
   Ono sideboard, he one
   Spinal cracker. He got
   Feet down below his knee.
   Hold you in his armchair you can feel his disease.

4. He roller coaster, he got
   Early warning. He got
   Muddy water, he one
   Mojo filter. He say,
   "One and one and one is three."
   Got to be good looking 'cause he so hard to see.

The Continuing Story of Bungalow Bill

Words and Music by John Lennon and Paul McCartney

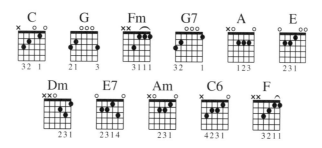

*Strum Pattern: 2
*Pick Pattern: 4

Chorus
Moderately

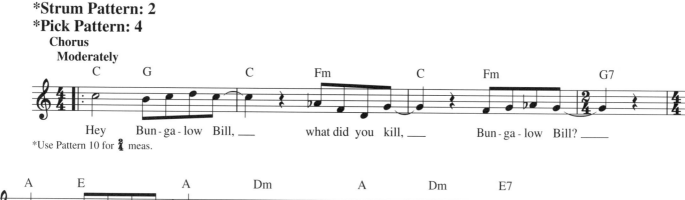

C   G   C   Fm   C   Fm   G7

Hey   Bun-ga-low Bill, ___   what did you   kill, ___   Bun-ga-low Bill? ___

*Use Pattern 10 for ⅔ meas.

A   E   A   Dm   A   Dm   E7

Hey   Bun-ga-low Bill, ___   what did you kill, ___   Bun-ga-low Bill? ___   1. He

Additional Lyrics

2. Deep in the jungle where the mighty tiger lies,
Bill and his elephants were taken by surprise.
So Captain Marvel zapped him right between the eyes.
All the children sing:

3. The children asked him if to kill was not a sin.
"Now when he looked so fierce," his mommy butted in,
"If looks could kill it would've been us instead of him."
All the children sing:

Day Tripper

Words and Music by John Lennon and Paul McCartney

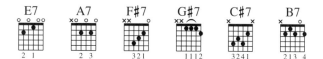

E7   A7   F#7   G#7   C#7   B7

Strum Pattern: 2, 5
Pick Pattern: 4

Intro
Moderate Rock

Verse

1. Got a good rea - son   for tak-ing the eas - y way out. ___
2., 3. *See additional lyrics*

Got a good rea - son   for tak-ing the eas - y way out, ___ now.   She was a

Chorus

day _____ trip-per, { 1., 2. one way   tick - et, }   yeah.   It took me
                          { 3. Sun-day   driv - er, }

To Coda

so _____ long ___ to find out, ___   and I found out.

Bridge   **Guitar Solo**
Play 3 times

out.

D.C. al Coda

Coda ⊕

Outro

B7

E7

Play 4 times

out.

Repeat and fade

Day   trip - per,   day   trip - per,   yeah.

Additional Lyrics

2. She's a big teaser.
   She took me half the way there.
   She's a big teaser.
   She took me half the way there, now.

3. Tried to please her.
   She only played one night stands.
   Tried to please her.
   She only played one night stands, now.

Dear Prudence

Words and Music by John Lennon and Paul McCartney

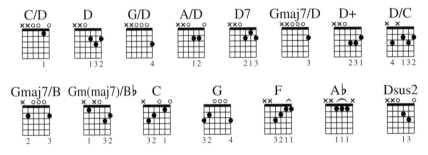

C/D   D   G/D   A/D   D7   Gmaj7/D   D+   D/C

Gmaj7/B   Gm(maj7)/B♭   C   G   F   A♭   Dsus2

Strum Pattern: 1
Pick Pattern: 5

Intro
Slowly

C/D   D   C/D   G/D   A/D   C/D   D   D7

※ Verse

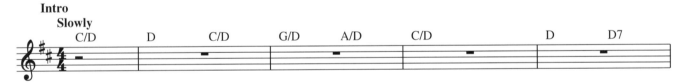

Gmaj7/D D+   D   D7   Gmaj7/D D+   D   D7

1. Dear ___ (4.) Pru-dence, _   won't you come out   to   play? ___
   2., 3. *See additional lyrics*

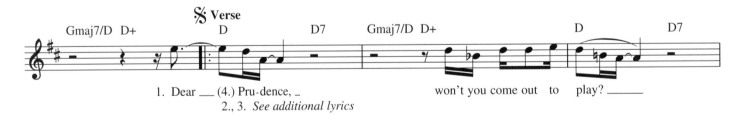

Gmaj7 D+   D   D7   Gmaj7/D D+   D   D7

Dear ___ Pru-dence, _   greet the brand new day. ___

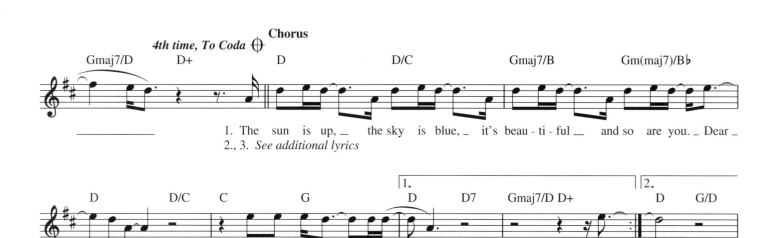

4th time, To Coda **Chorus**

1. The sun is up, __ the sky is blue, __ it's beau-ti-ful __ and so are you. __ Dear __
2., 3. *See additional lyrics*

__ Pru-dence, _ won't you come out __ to play? __ 2., 4. Dear __ __

Bridge

Look a-round, 'round, _ 'round _ 'round, 'round. 'Round, 'round, _ round, _ 'round, 'round.

'Round, 'round, _'round, _ 'round, 'round. 'Round, 'round, _'round, _ 'round, 'round. Look a-round.

D.S. al Coda (with repeats)

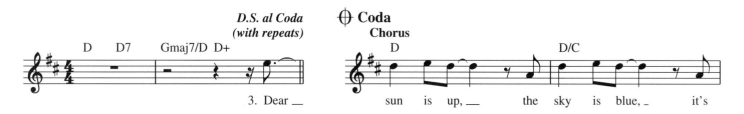

⊕ **Coda**
Chorus

3. Dear __ sun is up, __ the sky is blue, _ it's

beau-ti-ful, ____ and so are you. ____ Dear __ Pru-dence, _ won't you come out to

Outro

play? ____

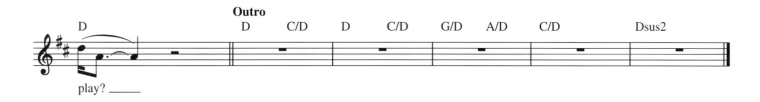

Additional Lyrics

2. Dear Prudence, open up your eyes.
Dear Prudence, see the sunny skies.

3. Dear Prudence, let me see you smile.
Dear Prudence, like a little child.

Chorus 2. The wind is low, the birds will sing,
That you are part of ev'rything.
Dear Prudence, won't you open up your eyes?

Chorus 3. The clouds will be a daisy chain,
So let me see you smile again.
Dear Prudence, won't you let me see you smile?

A Day in the Life

Words and Music by John Lennon and Paul McCartney

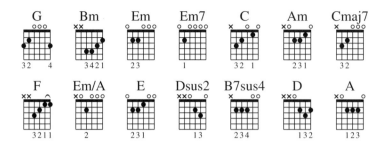

*Strum Pattern: 1
*Pick Pattern: 5

Intro
Slowly

*Use Pattern 9 for ⅜ meas.

Verse

1. I read the news to-day, _ oh boy, a-bout _ a luck-y man who made the grade.

And though the news _ was rath-er sad, well, I just had to laugh. _____

I saw the pho-to-graph. _____   2. He blew his mind out in _ a car.
                                          3., 5. *See additional lyrics*

He did-n't no-tice that the lights had changed.   A crowd of peo - ple stood and stared.

1.   *To Coda* ⊕

They'd seen his face be-fore; _ no-bod-y was real-ly sure if he was from the House of Lords. _

2.

hav-ing read the book.   I'd love to turn _____

Additional Lyrics

3. I saw a film today, oh boy.
   The English army had just won the war.
   A crowd of people turned away,
   But I just had to look; having read the book.
   I'd love to turn you on.

5. I read the news today, oh boy.
   Four thousand holes in Blackburn Lancashire.
   And though the holes were rather small,
   They had to count them all.
   Now they know how many holes it takes to fill the Albert Hall.
   I'd love to turn you on.

Do You Want to Know a Secret?

Words and Music by John Lennon and Paul McCartney

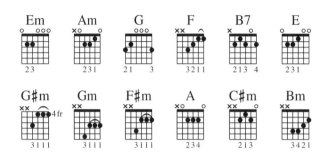

Strum Pattern: 4
Pick Pattern: 3

Intro
Rubato

You'll nev-er know how much I real-ly love you; you'll nev-er know how much I real-ly care.

𝄋 Chorus
Moderately

Lis-ten, do you want to know a se-cret? Do you prom-ise not to

tell? Whoa, _ whoa, ___ clos-er, let me whis-per in your ear;

To Coda ⊕

say the words you long to hear: _____ I'm _ in love with you. _ Ooh. ___

Bridge

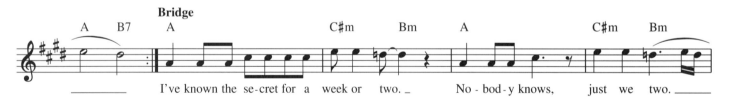

_____ I've known the se-cret for a week or two. _ No-bod-y knows, just we two. ___

D.S. al Coda   ⊕ **Coda**   **Outro**   *Repeat and fade*

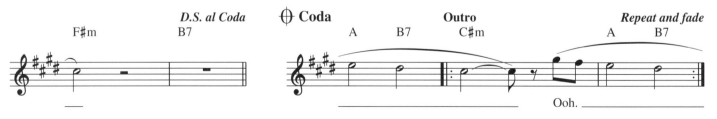

_____ Ooh.

Drive My Car

Words and Music by John Lennon and Paul McCartney

Strum Pattern: 3
Pick Pattern: 4

Intro
Moderately
N.C.

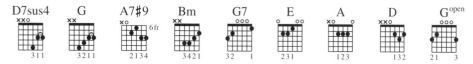

Verse

1. Asked a girl what she want-ed to be, ___ she said, "Ba-by, can't you see? ___
2., 4. *See additional lyrics* (3.) *Instrumental*

*3rd time, substitute D

I wan-na be fa-mous, a star of the screen, ___ but you can do some-thing in be - tween. ___

*sim.

Chorus

Ba - by you can drive my car. ___ Yes, I'm gon-na be a star. ___

1.
4th time, Coda

Ba - by, you can drive my car, ___ and may - be I'll love ___ you."

2.

___ you." Beep, beep, mm, beep, beep, yeah! ___

D.S. al Coda
(take repeat)

Coda

Outro

Repeat and fade

D   G   A7#9   D   G

___ you." Beep, beep, mm, beep, beep, yeah! ___

Additional Lyrics

2. I told that girl that my prospects were good.
She said, "Baby, it's understood,
Working for peanuts is all very fine,
But I can show you a better time."

4. I told that girl I could start right away,
And she said, "Listen babe, I got somethin' to say.
I got no car and it's breakin' my heart,
But I've found a driver, that's a start."

Don't Let Me Down

Words and Music by John Lennon and Paul McCartney

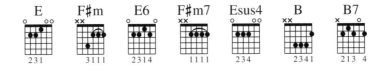

Bridge

time.

Don't you know it's gon-na last?

It's a love that lasts for-ev-er,

it's a love that had no

D.S. al Coda

Coda

past.

Don't let me

down. ____

Additional Lyrics

2. And from the first time that she really done me,
   Ooh, she done me, she done me good.
   I guess nobody ever really done me,
   Ooh, she done me, she does me good.

Eight Days a Week

Words and Music by John Lennon and Paul McCartney

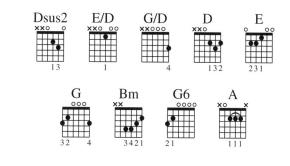

Strum Pattern: 6
Pick Pattern: 6

Intro
Brightly

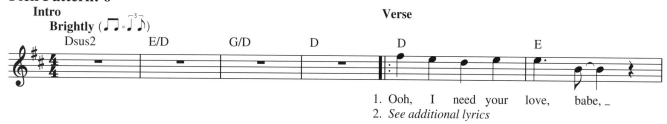

Verse

1. Ooh, I need your love, babe, ____
2. *See additional lyrics*

guess you know it's true. ____

Hope you need my love, babe, ____

just like I need you. ____

Additional Lyrics

2., 4. Love you ev'ry day, girl,
        Always on my mind.
        One thing I can say, girl,
        I love you all the time.

Eleanor Rigby

Words and Music by John Lennon and Paul McCartney

Strum Pattern: 6
Pick Pattern: 5

Intro
Moderately

Ah, _____ look at all _____ the lone - ly peo - ple! _____

Ah, _____ look at all _____ the lone - ly peo - ple! _____

1. El - ea - nor Rig - by,
2., 3. *See additional lyrics*

picks up the rice _ in the church _ where a wed - ding has been, _ lives in a dream. _

Waits at the win - dow, wear-ing a face _ that she keeps _ in a jar _ by the door, _

Chorus

who is it for? _____ All the lone - ly peo - ple, where do _____ they all _____ come from?

To Coda

_____ All the lone - ly peo - ple, where do _____ they all _____ be - long? _

1.

2.

D.C. al Coda

Coda

Additional Lyrics

2. Father McKenzie writing the words of a sermon that no one will hear,
No one comes near.
Look at him working, darning his socks in the night when there's nobody there,
What does he care?

3. Eleanor Rigby died in the church and was buried along with her name,
Nobody came.
Father McKenzie, wiping the dirt from his hands as he walks from the grave,
No one was saved.

Fixing a Hole

Words and Music by John Lennon and Paul McCartney

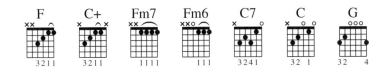

Strum Pattern: 5
Pick Pattern: 5

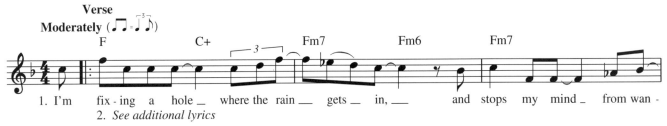

1. I'm fix-ing a hole __ where the rain __ gets __ in, __ and stops my mind __ from wan-
2. *See additional lyrics*

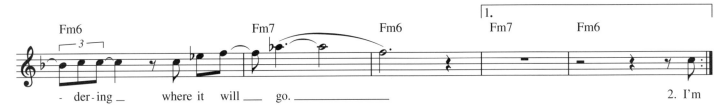

- der-ing __ where it will __ go. __ 2. I'm

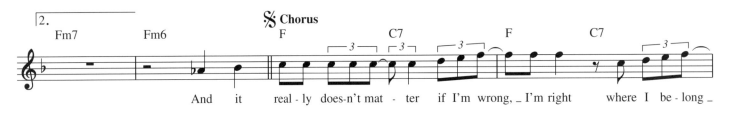

And it real-ly does-n't mat-ter if I'm wrong, __ I'm right where I be-long __

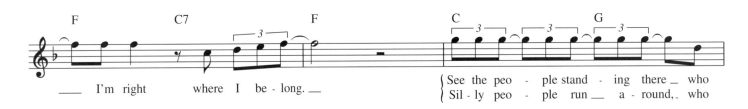

__ I'm right where I be-long. __

See the peo-ple stand-ing there __ who
Sil-ly peo-ple run a-round, __ who

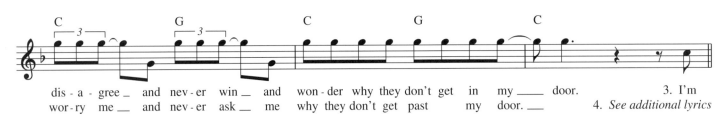

dis-a-gree __ and nev-er win and won-der why they don't get in my __ door. 3. I'm
wor-ry me __ and nev-er ask __ me why they don't get past my door. __ 4. *See additional lyrics*

Verse

paint-ing the room __ in a col-or-ful way, and when my mind __ is wan-

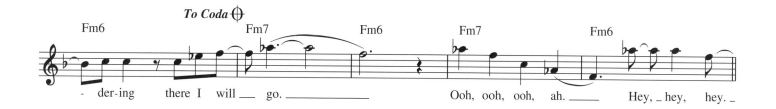

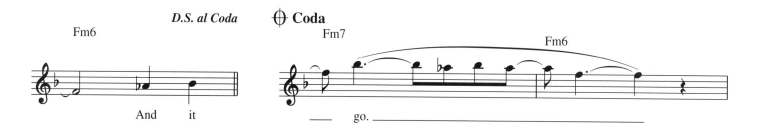

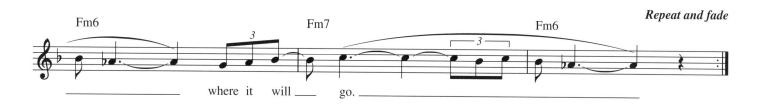

Additional Lyrics

2. I'm filling the cracks that ran through the door,
   And kept my mind from wandering where it will go.

4. I'm taking the time for a number of things,
   That weren't important yesterday and I still go.
   Ooh, ooh, ooh, ah.

Free As a Bird

Original Version: Words and Music by John Lennon
Beatles Version: Words and Music by John Lennon, Paul McCartney, George Harrison and Ringo Starr

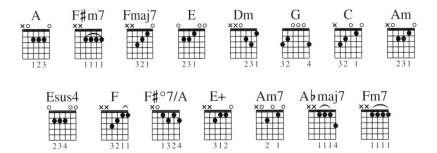

Strum Pattern: 4
Pick Pattern: 4

Intro
Moderately slow

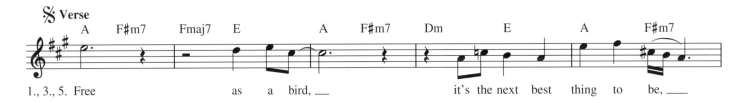

1., 3., 5. Free   as a bird, ___   it's the next best thing to be, ___

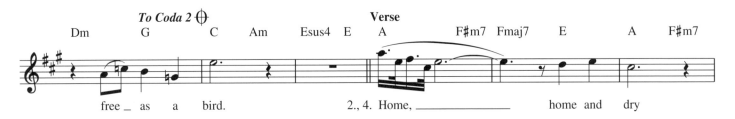

free _ as a bird.   2., 4. Home, _____ home and dry

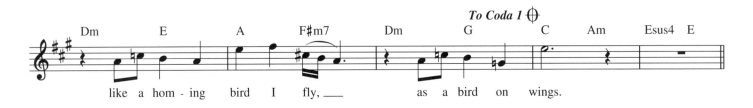

like a hom-ing bird I fly, ___   as a bird on wings.

Bridge

What-ev-er hap-pened to ___ the life that we once knew? Can we real-ly live with-

out each oth-er? Where did we lose _ the touch _ that seemed to mean _ so much?

D.S. al Coda 1 Coda 1

It al-ways made me feel so... ___   wing. ___

Bridge

What-ev-er hap-pened to the life that we once knew? Al-ways made me feel _

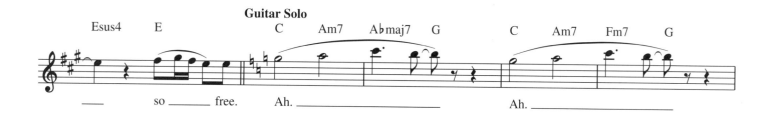

Guitar Solo

_ so ___ free. Ah. ___   Ah. ___

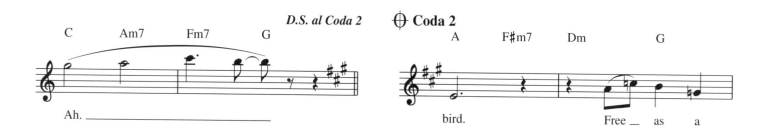

D.S. al Coda 2 Coda 2

Ah. ___   bird.   Free _ as a

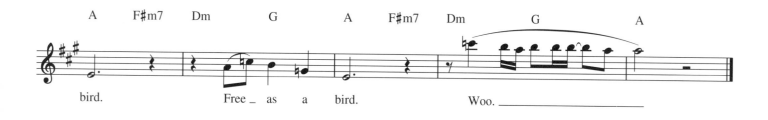

bird.   Free _ as a bird.   Woo. ___

Everybody's Got Something to Hide Except Me and My Monkey

Words and Music by John Lennon and Paul McCartney

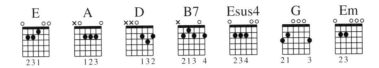

Strum Pattern: 2
Pick Pattern: 4

Intro
Moderately

E   A   E
Play 4 times

Come on, come on,   come on, come on. ___

% Chorus

E

Come on is such a joy,   come on is such a joy.   Come on let's {1., 3. take / 2. make} it eas-y,

A

come on let's {1., 3. take / 2. make} it eas-y.   Take it eas - y, ___   take it

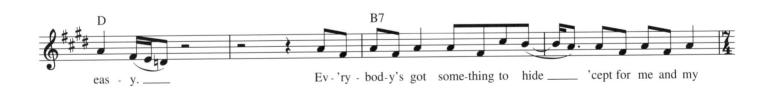

D   B7

eas - y. ___   Ev-'ry-bod-y's got some-thing to hide ___ 'cept for me and my

To Coda ⊕ Verse

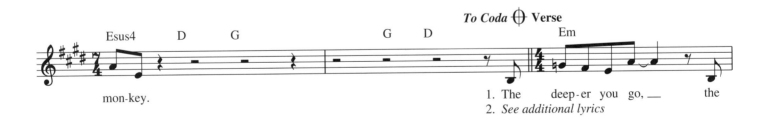

Esus4   D   G   G   D   Em

mon-key.

1. The deep-er you go, ___ the
2. *See additional lyrics*

high - er you fly. ____ The high - er you fly, ____ the deep - er you go, ____ so come on, ____

1.

2.

D.S. al Coda ⊕ **Coda**

E

E N.C.

come on. ____   *on. ____*

Outro   *Repeat and fade*

E   D   E

The Fool on the Hill

Words and Music by John Lennon and Paul McCartney

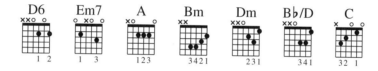

D6   Em7   A   Bm   Dm   B♭/D   C

Strum Pattern: 3
Pick Pattern: 4

Intro
Slowly
D6

Verse
D6   Em7

1. Day af - ter day,   a - lone on a hill; ____   the

D6

man with the fool - ish grin is keep - ing per - fect - ly still.   But

A   D6   Bm

no - bod - y wants to know _ him,   they can   see that he's just _   a   fool. ____   And

---

Additional Lyrics

2. Your inside is out when your outside is in.
Your outside is in when your inside is out,
So come on, come on.

1. Day af - ter day,
2. *See additional lyrics*

he nev - er gives an an - swer. But the fool ___ on the hill ___ sees the sun ___

Chorus

___ go-ing down _ and the eyes ___ in his head _ see the world _ spin-ning 'round. _

Interlude

Verse

3. No - bod - y seems to like _ him; they can tell what he wants _ to do. _____ And
4. *See additional lyrics*

he nev - er shows his feel - ings, but the fool ___ on the hill ___ sees the sun _

Chorus

___ go-ing down _ and the eyes ___ in his head _ see the world _ spin-ning 'round. _

Outro *Repeat and fade*

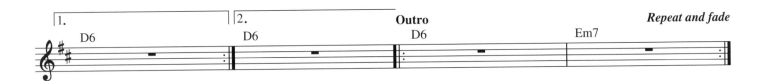

Additional Lyrics

2. Well on the way, head in a cloud;
The man of a thousand voices talking perfectly loud.
But nobody ever hears him, or the sound he appears to make.
And he never seems to notice.

4. He never listens to them
He knows that they're the fools,
They don't like him.

From Me to You

Words and Music by John Lennon and Paul McCartney

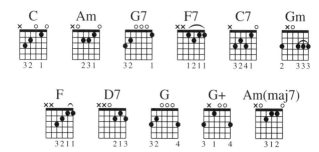

Strum Pattern: 6
Pick Pattern: 4

call on me ___ and I'll send it a - long ___ with love, ___ from me ___ to you.

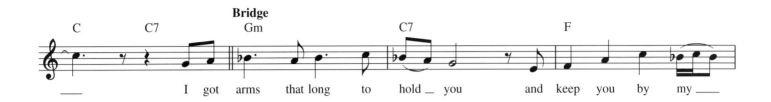

Bridge

___ I got arms that long to hold ___ you and keep you by my ___

D.S. al Coda 2

side. I got lips that long to kiss ___ you and keep you sat - is - fied, ooh. 4. If there's

Coda 2

___ to you, ___ to you, ___ to you.

Get Back

Words and Music by John Lennon and Paul McCartney

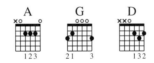

Strum Pattern: 1
Pick Pattern: 2

Intro
Moderate Rock

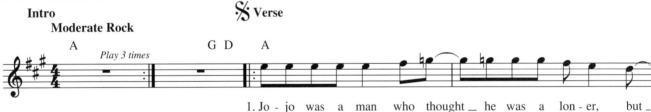

1. Jo - jo was a man who thought ___ he was a lon - er, but ___
2. *See additional lyrics*
3. *Instrumental*

___ he knew it could-n't last. ___ Jo - jo left his home in Tuc - son, Ar - i - zo - na, for ___

Additional Lyrics

2. Sweet Loretta Martin thought she was a woman,
   But she was another man.
   All the girls around her say she's got it comin',
   But she gets it while she can.

Girl

Words and Music by John Lennon and Paul McCartney

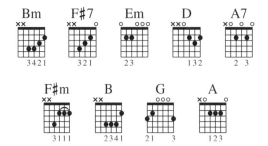

Strum Pattern: 2
Pick Pattern: 4

1. Is there an-y-bod-y going to lis-ten to my sto-ry
2., 3. *See additional lyrics*

all a-bout the girl who came to stay? She's the kind of girl you want so much it

makes you sor-ry, still you don't re-gret a sin-gle day. Ah,

girl. _____ Girl, girl. _____ 2. When I

She's the kind of girl who puts you down when friends are there, you feel a fool. _____

When you say she's look-ing good, she acts as if it's un-der-stood, she's

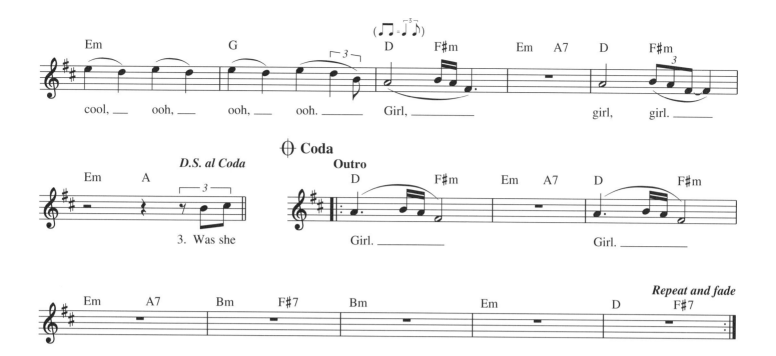

cool, ___ ooh, ___ ooh, ___ ooh. ___ Girl, ___ girl, girl. ___

$\oplus$ **Coda**

D.S. al Coda   **Outro**

3. Was she   Girl. ___   Girl. ___

Repeat and fade

Additional Lyrics

2. When I think of all the times I tried so hard to leave her
   She will turn to me and start to cry.
   And she promises the earth to me and I believe her,
   After all this time I don't know why.

3. Was she told when she was young that pain would lead to pleasure?
   Did she understand it when they said
   That a man must break his back to earn his day of leisure?
   Will she still believe it when she's dead?

Give Peace a Chance

Words and Music by John Lennon

Strum Pattern: 3, 1
Pick Pattern: 2, 3

Verse
Moderately

C

1. *Spoken: Everybody's   talking   about   Bagism,   Shagism,   Dragism,   Madism,*
2., 3., 4. *See additional lyrics*

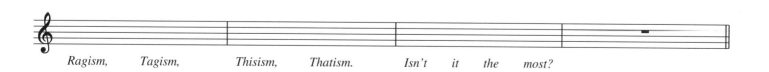

Ragism,   Tagism,   Thisism,   Thatism.   Isn't   it   the   most?

Chorus

All we ___ are say - ing   is give peace ___ a

chance.   All we ___ are say -

ing   is give peace ___ a chance.

1.   2.   3.

C' - mon.   Let me tell you now.   Oh, let's stick to it.

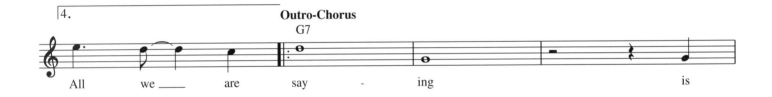

4.   **Outro-Chorus**

All we ___ are say - ing   is

Repeat and fade

give peace ___ a chance.   All we ___ are

Additional Lyrics

2. Spoken: Ev'rybody's talking about Ministers, Sinisters,
     Banisters and Canisters,
     Bishops and Fishops,
     Rabbis and Popeyes. Bye, bye, bye byes.

3. Spoken: Ev'rybody's talking about Revolution, Evolution,
     Mastication, Flagellation,
     Regulations, Integrations,
     Meditations, United Nations, Congratulations.

4. Spoken: Ev'rybody's talking about John and Yoko, Timmy Leary,
     Rosemary, Tommy Smothers, Bobby Dylan, Tommy Cooper,
     Derek Taylor, Norman Mailer, Alan Ginsberg, Hare Krishna;
     Hare, Hare Krishna.

Good Day Sunshine

Words and Music by John Lennon and Paul McCartney

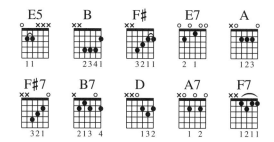

*Strum Pattern: 2
* Pick Pattern: 4

Intro
Moderately

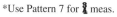
*Use Pattern 7 for ½ meas.

§ Chorus

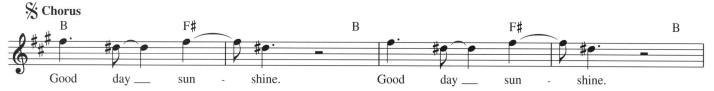

Good day __ sun - shine. Good day __ sun - shine.

Verse

Good day __ sun - shine. 1. I need to laugh and when the sun is out __
2. *See additional lyrics*

I've got some-thing I can laugh a-bout. I feel good __ in a spe-cial way. __

Chorus

I'm in love and it's a sun-ny day. __ Good day __ sun - shine.

To Coda ⊕

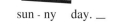

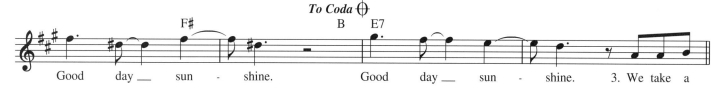

Good day __ sun - shine. Good day __ sun - shine. 3. We take a

Verse

walk, the sun is shin-ing down; burns my feet as they touch __ the ground. __

Interlude

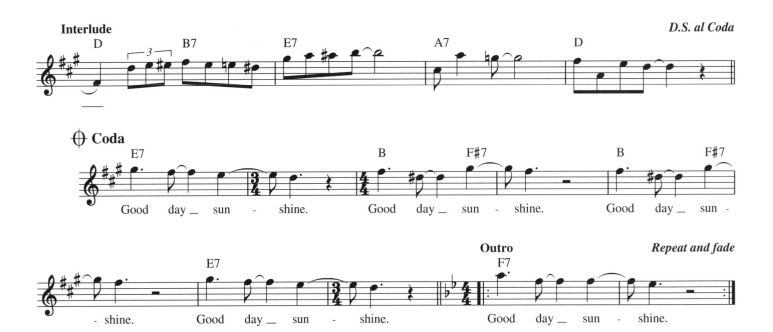

⊕ Coda

Good day __ sun - shine. Good day __ sun - shine. Good day __ sun

Outro *Repeat and fade*

- shine. Good day __ sun - shine. Good day __ sun - shine.

Additional Lyrics

2. Then we'd lie beneath a shady tree,
   I love her and she's loving me.
   She feels good, she knows she's looking fine.
   I'm so proud to know that she is mine.

Got to Get You Into My Life

Words and Music by John Lennon and Paul McCartney

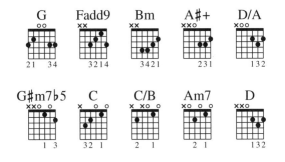

Strum Pattern: 2
Pick Pattern: 4

Intro
Moderately

N.C.

§ Verse
G   Fadd9

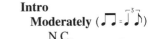

1. I was a - lone, __ I took a ride, __ I did-n't know __ what I would find __ there. __
2., 3. *See additional lyrics*

An - oth - er road, _ where may-be I _____ could see an - oth - er kind of mind _ there. _

Ooh, then I sud - den - ly see _ you. Ooh, _ did I tell _____ you I need _ you

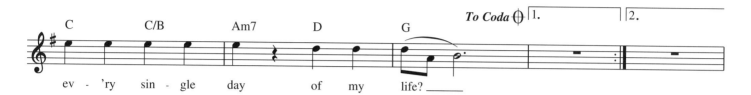

ev - 'ry sin - gle day of my life? _____

Got to get you in - to my life! _____

D.S. al Coda   ⊕ **Coda**

Got to get you in - to my life! _

Got to get you in - to my life! _____

Outro

Got to get you in - to my life! _____

Additional Lyrics

2. You didn't run, you didn't lie,
   You knew I wanted just to hold you.
   And had you gone you knew in time
   We'd meet again for I'd have told you.
   Ooh, you were meant to be near me.
   Ooh, and I want you to hear me
   Say we'll be together ev'ryday.
   Got to get you into my life!

3. What can I do, what can I be,
   When I'm with you I want to stay there.
   If I am true I'll never leave
   And if I do I know the way there.
   Ooh, then I suddenly see you.
   Ooh, did I tell you I need you
   Ev'ry single day of my life?
   Got to get you into my life!

A Hard Day's Night

Words and Music by John Lennon and Paul McCartney

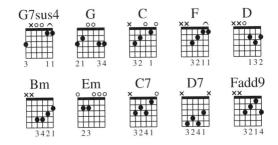

Strum Pattern: 2
Pick Pattern: 4

Verse

4. So why on earth should I moan _ 'cause when I get you a - lone _ you know I

D.S.S. al Coda 2   **Coda 2**

feel _ o - kay. _ When I'm home _ _ yeah. _ 5. It's been a

Verse

hard day's night, _ and I been work - in' _ like a dog. _ It's been a

hard day's night, _ I should be sleep - in' _ like a log. _ But when I

get home to you _ I find the things that you do _ will make me feel _ al - right. _

Outro   *Play 3 times and fade*

_ You know I feel _ al - right. _ You know I feel al - right. _

Additional Lyrics

2. You know I work all day,
   To get you money to buy your things.
   And it's worth it just to hear you say
   You're gonna give me ev'rything.
   So why on earth should I moan
   'Cause when I get you alone
   You know I feel okay.

Hello, Goodbye

Words and Music by John Lennon and Paul McCartney

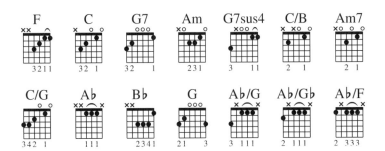

*Strum Pattern: 2
*Pick Pattern: 4

Verse
Moderately

1. You say yes, __ I say no. __ You say stop __ and I say go, __ go, go.

*Use Pattern 10 for 2/4 meas.

Oh, __ no. __ You say _ good-bye _ and I say hel-lo, __

hel-lo, __ hel-lo. __ I don't _ know why you say good-bye, _ I say hel-lo, __

hel-lo, __ hel-lo. __ I don't _ know why you say good-bye, _ I say hel-lo. __

Verse

2. I say high, __ you say low; __ you say why, __ and I say I __ don't know.
4. You say yes, __ I say no; __ you say stop, __ and I say go, __ go, go. __

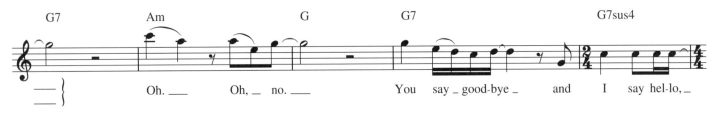

Oh. __ Oh, __ no. __ You say _ good-bye _ and I say hel-lo, __

hel-lo, __ hel-lo. __ I don't __ know why you say good-bye, _ I say hel-lo, _

To Coda ⊕

hel-lo, __ hel-lo. __ I don't __ know why you say good-bye, _ I say hel-lo. _

Verse

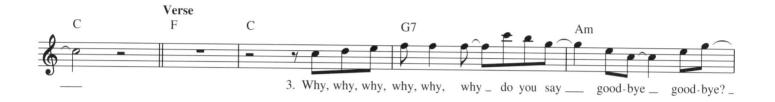

3. Why, why, why, why, why, why _ do you say __ good-bye _ good-bye? _

Oh, __ no. __ You say _ good-bye _ and I say hel-lo, _

hel-lo, __ hel-lo, __ I don't __ know why you say good-bye, _ I say hel-lo, _

D.S. al Coda

hel-lo, __ hel-lo. __ I don't __ know why you say good-bye, _ I say hel-lo. _

⊕ **Coda**

Hel-lo, __ hel-lo, __ I don't __ know why you say good-bye, _ I say hel-lo. _

Outro

Repeat and fade

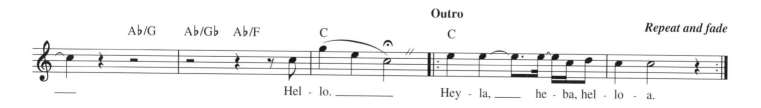

Hel-lo. __ Hey - la, __ he - ba, hel - lo - a.

Help!

Words and Music by John Lennon and Paul McCartney

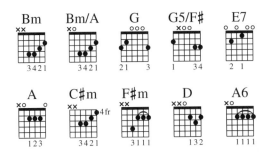

Strum Pattern: 3, 4
Pick Pattern: 1, 3

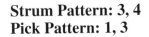

Moderately

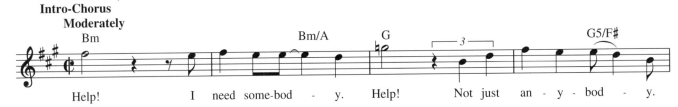

Help! I need some-bod-y. Help! Not just an-y-bod-y.

Help! You know I need some-one. _ Help! _____ 1., 3. When I ____ was
2. *See additional lyrics*

young-er, so ___ much young-er than _ to-day, _____ I nev-er need-ed

an-y-bod-y's help in an-y way. _ But now these days are gone, _ I'm

not so self-as-sured. _____ Now I find I've changed my mind, _ I've

o-pened up the doors. _ Help me if you can, _ I'm feel-ing down. _

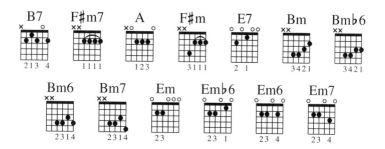

And I do ___ ap- pre- ci- ate ___ you be- ing 'round. ___

Help me get ___ my feet ___ back on the ground. ___ Won't you please

please ___ help ___ me? ___ ___ Help me, help me! ___ Ooh.

Additional Lyrics

2. And now my life has changed in, oh, so many ways;
   My independence seems to vanish in the haze.
   But ev'ry now and then I feel so insecure.
   I know that I just need you like I've never done before.

Hey Bulldog

Words and Music by John Lennon and Paul McCartney

Strum Pattern: 2
Pick Pattern: 4

Intro

Moderately slow

N.C.(B)

Play 3 times

§ Verse

1. Sheep- dog   stand- ing in the rain;   bull- frog   do- ing it a- gain.
2., 3. *See additional lyrics*

Some kind of hap- pi- ness ___ is meas- ured out in miles.   What makes you think you're some- thing

spe - cial when you smile? _____ lis - ten to your fears. _____ You can talk _____ to me, _____

you can talk to me. _____ You can talk to me, if you're lone - ly you can talk to me.

To Coda ⊕ **Interlude**

D.S. al Coda
(take 2nd ending)

⊕ **Coda**

Repeat and fade

Outro

Hey, Bull - dog. _____ Hey, Bull - dog.

Additional Lyrics

2. Childlike, no one understands;
   Jackknife in your sweaty hands.
   Some kind of innocence is measured out in years,
   You don't know what it's like to listen to your fears.

3. Big man waiting in the dark;
   Wigwam, frightened of the dark.
   Some kind of solitude is measured out in you.
   You think you know me but you haven't got a clue.

Helter Skelter

Words and Music by John Lennon and Paul McCartney

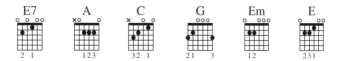

Strum Pattern: 3
Pick Pattern: 3

Intro
Moderate Rock

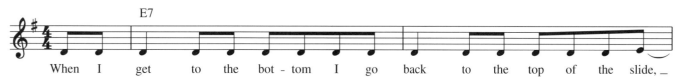

When I get to the bot-tom I go back to the top of the slide, __

__ where I stop and I turn, and I go for a ride, ___ till I get to the

bot-tom and I see you a-gain. ___ Yeah, yeah, yeah, yeah.

Verse

1. But do you, don't you want me to love you? I'm

com-ing down fast but I'm miles a-bove __ you.

Tell me, tell me, tell __ me, come on tell me the an-swer. ___ Well you

may - be a lov-er but you ain't no ___ danc - er. ___ Now

Chorus

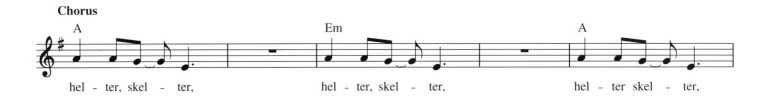

hel - ter, skel - ter,   hel - ter, skel - ter,   hel - ter skel - ter,

𝄋 **Verse**

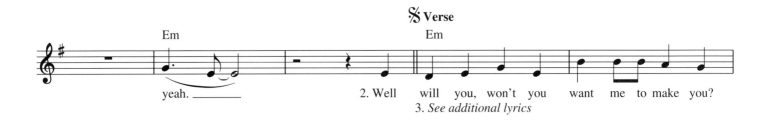

yeah. ___   2. Well will you, won't you want me to make you?
3. *See additional lyrics*

I'm com-ing down fast but don't let me break you.

Tell me, tell me, tell me the an - swer. You may be a lov - er but you

Chorus

ain't no danc - er.   Look out! ___   Hel - ter, skel - ter,

To Coda ⊕

hel - ter, skel - ter,   hel - ter, skel - ter,

Bridge

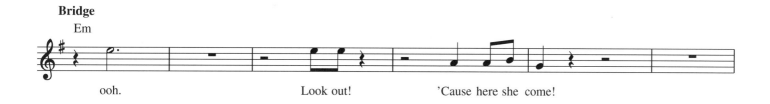

ooh.   Look out!   'Cause here she come!

When I

get   to   the bot-tom, I   go   back   to   the   top   of   the   slide, _____ and I   stop   and   I

turn,   and   I   go   for   a   ride _____   and   I   get   to   the   bot-tom and   I   see   you a-gain.

D.S. al Coda

_____   Yeah, yeah,   yeah,   yeah.   3. Well

Fade out

⊕ Coda

Spoken: Look out! Helter skelter! She's coming down fast. Yes, she is.

Additional Lyrics

3. Well do you, don't you want me to make you?
   I'm coming down fast but don't let me break you.
   Tell me, tell me, tell me the answer.
   You may be a lover but you ain't no dancer.

Her Majesty

Words and Music by John Lennon and Paul McCartney

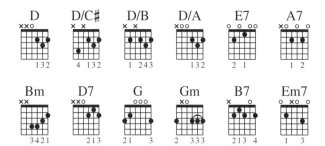

Strum Pattern: 6
Pick Pattern: 4

Moderately

Her Maj - es - ty's a pret - ty nice girl, but she

does - n't have a lot to say. ____ Her Maj - es - ty's a

pret - ty nice girl, but she chang - es from day ____ to day. ____

I wan - na tell her that I love her a lot, ____ but I got - ta get a bel - ly full of

wine. Her Maj - es - ty's a pret - ty nice girl, some day ____

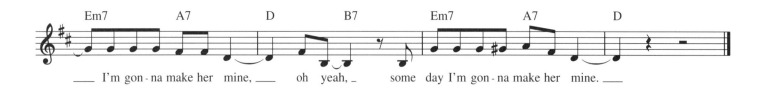

____ I'm gon - na make her mine, ____ oh yeah, __ some day I'm gon - na make her mine. ____

I Am the Walrus

Words and Music by John Lennon and Paul McCartney

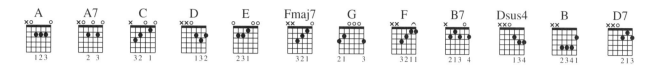

Strum Pattern: 4
Pick Pattern: 5

Verse
Moderate Rock

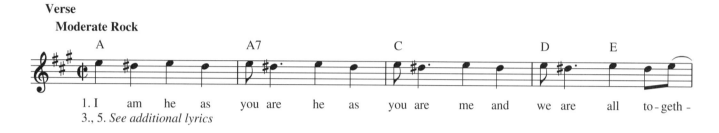

1. I am he as you are he as you are me and we are all to-geth-
3., 5. *See additional lyrics*

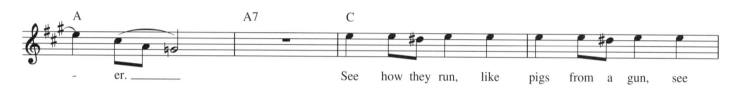

-er. ___ See how they run, like pigs from a gun, see

To Coda 1

how __ they fly. __ I'm cry-ing. __

Verse

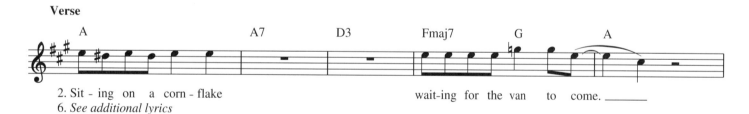

2. Sit-ing on a corn-flake   wait-ing for the van to come. _____
6. *See additional lyrics*

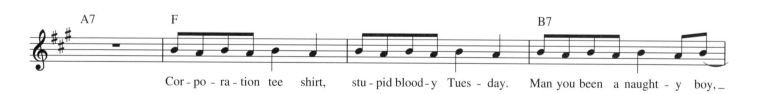

Cor-po-ra-tion tee shirt, stu-pid blood-y Tues-day. Man you been a naught-y boy,__

Chorus

__ you let your face grow long. __   I am the egg-man.

Ooh.   They are   the   egg - men.   Ooh.   I   am   the   wal - rus,   goo, goo,   g' joob.

⊕ **Coda 1**

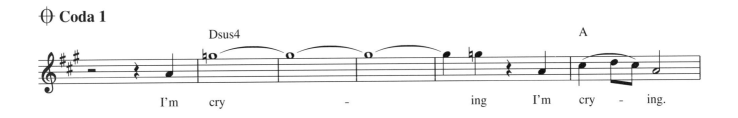

I'm   cry   -   ing   I'm   cry - ing.

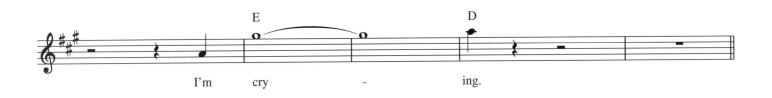

I'm   cry   -   ing.

Verse

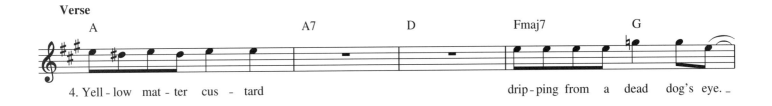

4. Yell - low   mat - ter   cus - tard   drip - ping   from   a   dead   dog's   eye. _

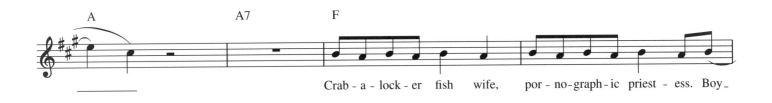

_____   Crab - a - lock - er   fish   wife,   por - no - graph - ic   priest - ess.   Boy _

_ you   been   a   naugh - ty   girl, _   you   let   your   knick - ers   down. _   I   am   the

Chorus

egg - man.   Ooh.   They   are   the   egg - men.   Ooh.   I   am   the

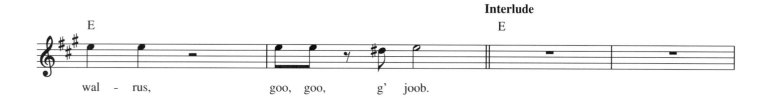

wal - rus,   goo, goo,   g' joob.

Bridge

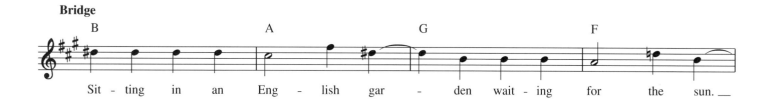

Sit - ting in an Eng - lish gar - den wait - ing for the sun. ___

___   If the sun don't come, ___ you get a tan from stand -

- ing in the Eng - lish rain. ___   I am the

Chorus

egg - man   They are the egg - men.   I am the

D.C. al Coda 2

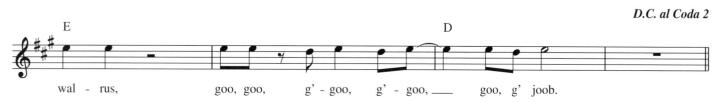

wal - rus,   goo, goo,   g' - goo, g' - goo, ___ goo, g' joob.

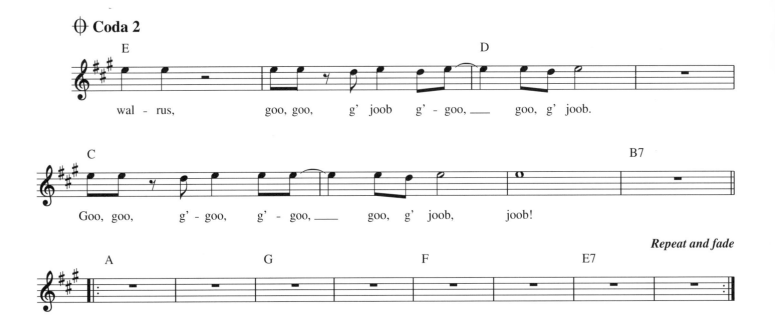

wal - rus, goo, goo, g' joob g' - goo, ___ goo, g' joob.

Goo, goo, g' - goo, g' - goo, ___ goo, g' joob, joob!

Repeat and fade

Additional Lyrics

3. Mister city p'liceman sitting pretty little p'licemen in a row.
   See how they fly like Lucy in the sky, see how they run.
   I'm crying.

5. Expert texpert choking smokers, don't you think the joker laughs at you?
   See how they smile, like pigs in a sty, see how they hide.
   I'm crying.

6. Semolina pilchards climbing up the Eiffel Tower.
   Element'ry penguin singing Hare Krishna.
   Man, you should have seen them kicking Edgar Allen Poe.

I Feel Fine

Words and Music by John Lennon and Paul McCartney

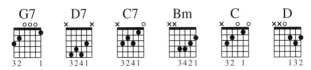

Strum Pattern: 2, 6
Pick Pattern: 4

Additional Lyrics

2., 3. Baby says she's mine, you know,
She tells me all the time,
You know, she said so.
I'm in love with her and I feel fine.

Here Comes the Sun

Words and Music by George Harrison

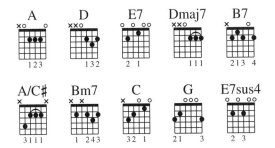

Strum Pattern: 2
Pick Pattern: 4

Intro
Moderately

Here comes _ the sun, _

_ doo, da, doo, doo.   Here comes _ the sun, _ and I say, "It's all _ right."

1. Lit - tle dar - ling,
2., 3. *See additional lyrics*

it's been _ a long, _ cold, lone - ly win - ter.   Lit - tle dar - ling,

it feels _ like years _ since it's _ been here. _   Here comes _ the sun. _

To Coda

D.S. al Coda

Coda

Here comes the sun, and I say, "It's all right."

Sun, sun, sun, here it comes.

Here comes the sun. Here comes the sun.

It's all right. It's all right.

Additional Lyrics

2. Little darling,
The smiles returning to their faces.
Little darling,
It seems like years since it's been here.

3. Little darling,
I feel that ice is slowly melting.
Little darling,
It seems like years since it's been clear.

Here, There and Everywhere

Words and Music by John Lennon and Paul McCartney

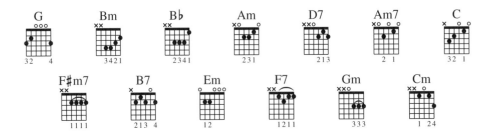

Strum Pattern: 3
Pick Pattern: 3

Intro
Slowly

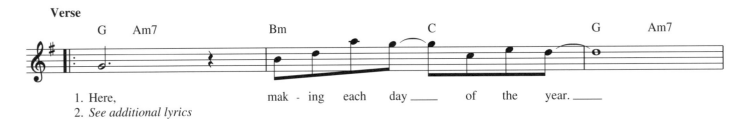

To lead a bet-ter life, I need my love to be here. ___

Verse

1. Here, mak-ing each day ___ of the year. ___
2. *See additional lyrics*

Chang-ing my life ___ with a wave ___ of her hand. _ No-bo-dy can ___ de-ny ___

___ that there's some - thing there. ___ ___ I want her

Bridge

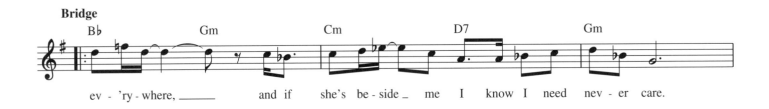

ev - 'ry-where, ___ and if she's be-side _ me I know I need nev-er care.

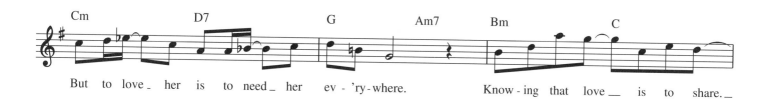

But to love her is to need her ev - 'ry-where. Know - ing that love is to share.

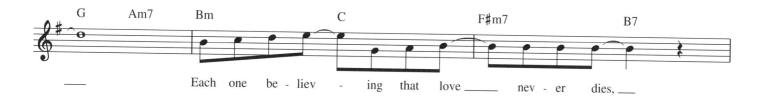

Each one be - liev - ing that love nev - er dies,

watch - ing her eyes and hop - ing I'm al - ways there. I want her

2.

Outro

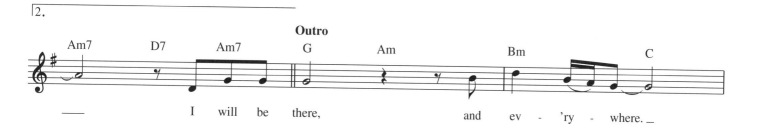

I will be there, and ev - 'ry - where.

Here, there and ev - 'ry - where.

Additional Lyrics

2. There, running my hands through her hair.
   Both of us thinking how good it can be.
   Someone is speaking,
   But she doesn't know he's there.

Hey Jude

Words and Music by John Lennon and Paul McCartney

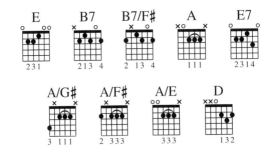

Strum Pattern: 2
Pick Pattern: 4

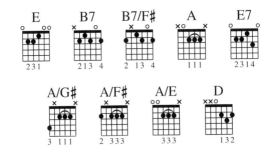

Verse
Rock Ballad

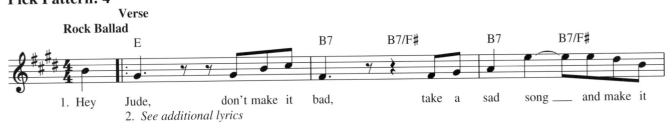

1. Hey   Jude,   don't make it bad,   take a sad   song ___ and make it
2. *See additional lyrics*

bet - ter. _____   Re - mem-ber to let her in - to your heart,   then you can start _

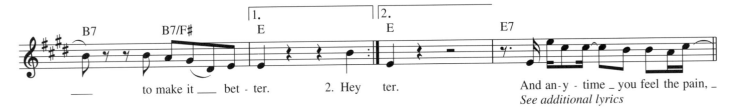

___   to make it ___ bet - ter.   2. Hey   ter.   And an-y - time _ you feel the pain, _
See additional lyrics

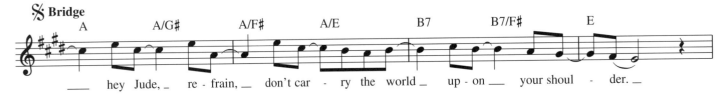

Bridge

___ hey Jude, _ re - frain, _ don't car - ry the world _ up - on ___ your shoul - der. _

For well, you know _ that it's a fool ___ who plays _   it cool ___ by mak - ing his world _

___ a lit - tle cold - er. _   Na, na, na,   na, _ na,   na, na, na,   na.

Additional Lyrics

2. Hey Jude, don't be afraid,
You were made to go out and get her.
The minute you let her under your skin,
Then you begin to make it better.

Bridge So let it out and let it in,
Hey Jude, begin,
You're waiting for someone to perform with.
And don't you know that it's just you?
Hey Jude, you'll do, the movement you need
Is on your shoulder. Na, na, na, na, na, na, na, na, na.

I Saw Her Standing There

Words and Music by John Lennon and Paul McCartney

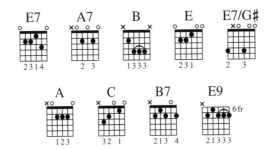

Strum Pattern: 2
Pick Pattern: 4

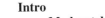

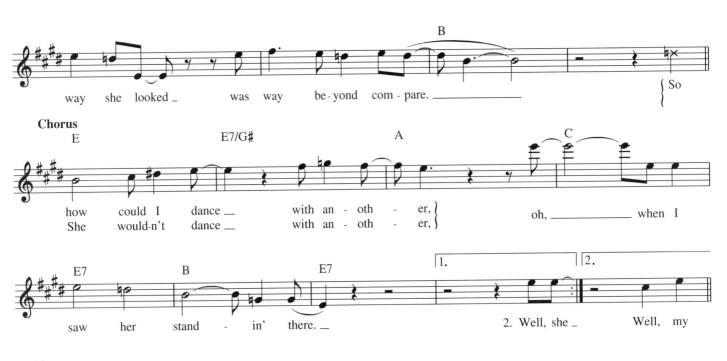

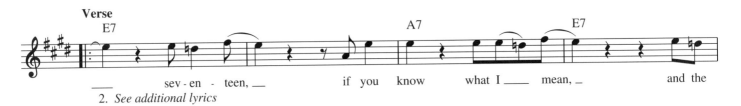

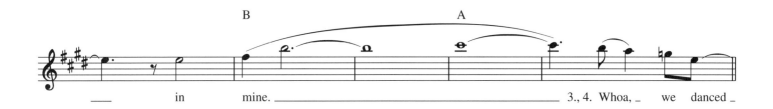

in mine. _____ 3., 4. Whoa, _ we danced _

Verse

____ through the night ___ and we held each oth-er tight, ___ and be -

fore too long ___ I fell in love ___ with her. _____ Now,

Chorus

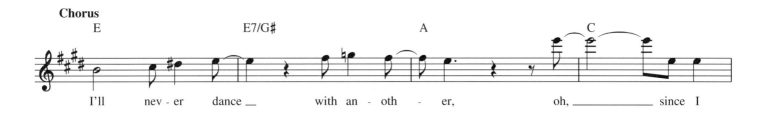

I'll nev-er dance ___ with an-oth-er, oh, _____ since I

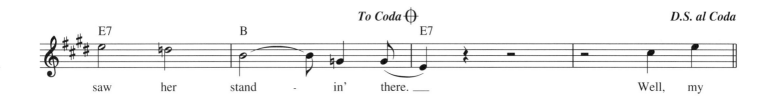

To Coda ⊕   *D.S. al Coda*

saw her stand - in' there. ___ Well, my

⊕ **Coda**

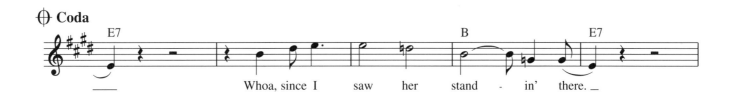

____ Whoa, since I saw her stand - in' there. ___

Yeah, well, since I saw her stand - in' there. ___

Additional Lyrics

2. Well, she looked at me
And I, I could see
That before too long
I'd fall in love with her.

I Want to Hold Your Hand

Words and Music by John Lennon and Paul McCartney

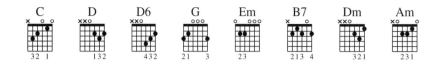

Intro
Moderately fast

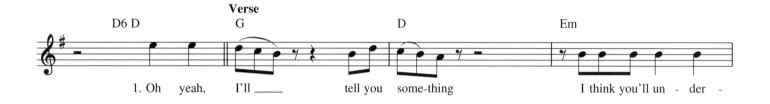

Verse

1. Oh yeah, I'll ____ tell you some-thing I think you'll un - der -

stand. When I ____ say that some - thing, I wan - na hold your hand. _

Chorus

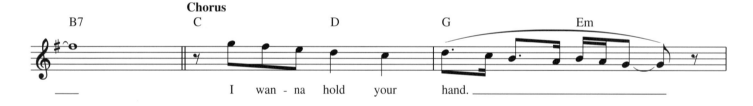

____ I wan - na hold your hand. _____

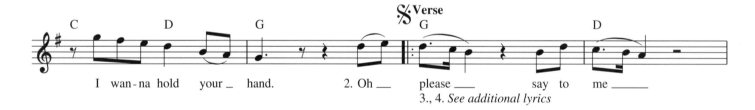

I wan - na hold your _ hand. 2. Oh ____ please ____ say to me ____
3., 4. *See additional lyrics*

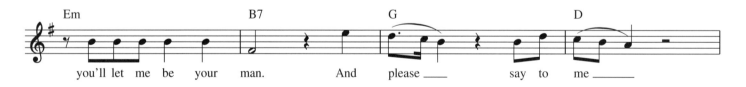

you'll let me be your man. And please ____ say to me ____

To Coda ⊕ **Chorus**

you'll let me hold your hand. _ Now, let me hold your hand. _____

I wan - na hold your _ hand. And when I touch you I feel

hap - py in - side. ___ It's such a feel - ing that my

love, I can't hide, ___ I can't hide, ___ I can't hide.

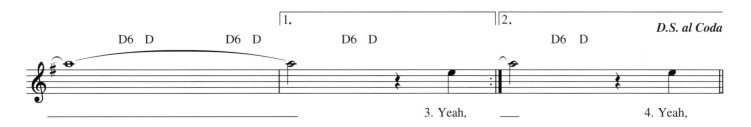

3. Yeah, ___ 4. Yeah,

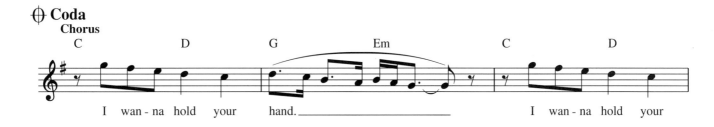

I wan - na hold your hand. ___ I wan - na hold your

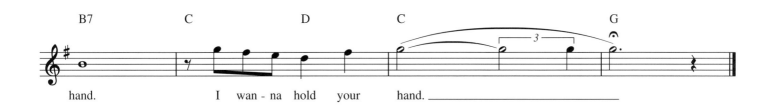

hand. I wan - na hold your hand. ___

Additional Lyrics

3. Yeah, you got that somethin',
   I think you'll understand.
   When I say that something,
   I wanna hold your hand.

4. Yeah, you got that somethin',
   I think you'll understand.
   When I feel that something,
   I wanna hold your hand.

I Want You
(She's So Heavy)

Words and Music by John Lennon and Paul McCartney

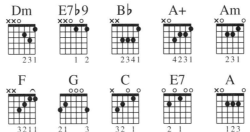

*Strum Pattern: 8
*Pick Pattern: 8

*Use Pattern 10 for $\frac{2}{4}$ meas. & Pattern 2 for $\frac{4}{4}$ meas.

1. I want (2., 3., 4.) you. I want you so bad. I want you. I want you so bad, it's driv-ing me mad, it's driv-ing me mad. I want you. I want you so bad, babe. I want you. I want you so bad, it's driv-ing me mad, it's driv-ing me mad.

2. I want She's so

I'll Cry Instead

Words and Music by John Lennon and Paul McCartney

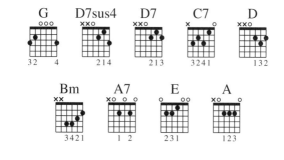

Strum Pattern: 3, 4
Pick Pattern: 1, 3

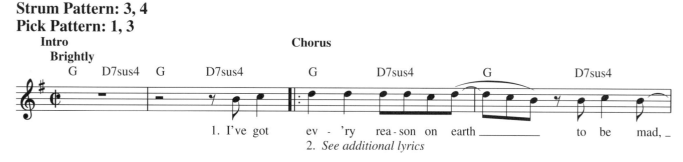

and if I _____ could get my way, _____ I'd get my-self locked

up to-day._ But I can't, _ so I'll cry _____ in - stead.

2. I've got a

Chorus

Don't want to cry when there's peo-ple there; _ I get shy when they start to stare, _

_____ I'm gon-na hide my-self a - way, _____ hey, _____ but I'll come back a -

gain some day. _ And when I do you'd bet-ter hide _____ all the girls, _

'cause I'm gon-na break their hearts _ all 'round the world. _

Yes,

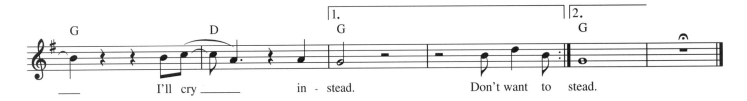

I'm gon-na break 'em in two, _ I'll show you what your lov-in' man _ can do. _ Un-til then _

_____ I'll cry _____ in - stead.

Don't want to stead.

Additional Lyrics

2. I've got a chip on my shoulder
That's bigger than my feet,
I can't talk to people that I meet.
If I could see you now,
I'd try to make you sad somehow,
But I can't, so I'll cry instead.

I'll Follow the Sun

Words and Music by John Lennon and Paul McCartney

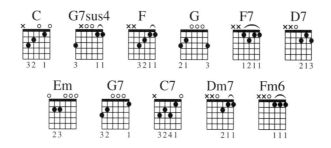

I've Just Seen a Face

Words and Music by John Lennon and Paul McCartney

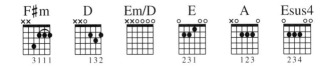

Strum Pattern: 2, 3
Pick Pattern: 2, 4

Intro
Brightly

place where we just met. She's just the girl ___ for me and I _____ want all the

world to see ___ we've met. Mm, mm, mm, mm, ___ mm.

Verse

2. Had it been ___ an-oth-er day ___ I might have looked the oth-er way ___ and
3. *See additional lyrics*
4. *Instrumental*

I'd have nev-er been __ a-ware. __ But as it is I'll dream of her __ to-night. __

__ Da, da, da, da, da, da. __

Chorus

Fall - ing, __ yes, I am fall - ing, __ and she keeps call - ing __

1., 2.   3.   *D.S. al Coda*

me back a - gain. __ gain. __

Coda

Outro

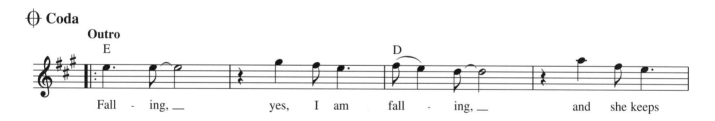

Fall - ing, __ yes, I am fall - ing, __ and she keeps

1., 2.

call - ing __ me back a - gain. __

3.   N.C.   A

gain.

Additional Lyrics

3. I have never known the like of this;
   I've been alone and I have missed things and kept out of sight.
   For other girls were never quite like this.
   Da, da, da, da, da, da.

If I Fell

Words and Music by John Lennon and Paul McCartney

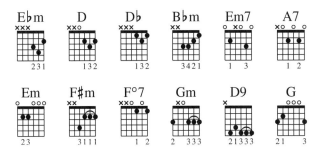

Strum Pattern: 3, 4
Pick Pattern: 1, 3

Intro
Moderately

If I fell in love with you would you prom-ise to be true and help me

un-der-stand? 'Cause I've been in love be-fore and I found that love was more than

just hold-ing hands. 1. If I give my heart to you, I
2. *See additional lyrics*

must be sure from the ver-y start that you would love me more than

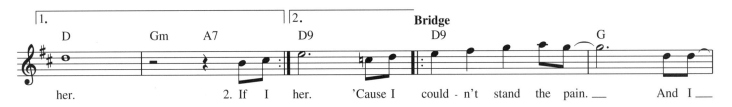

her.   2. If I her. 'Cause I could-n't stand the pain. And I

would be sad if our new love was in vain. 3., 4. So I

hope   you   see   that   I   would   love   to   love   you   and   that

she   will   cry   when   she   learns   we   are   two. ___   'Cause I

she learns we are two. __   If   I   fell   in   love   with   you.

Additional Lyrics

2. If I trust in you, oh,
Please don't run and hide if I love you, too.
Oh, please don't hurt my pride like her.

If I Needed Someone

Words and Music by George Harrison

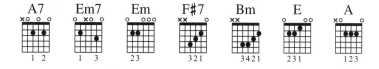

Strum Pattern: 6
Pick Pattern: 4

Intro
Moderately

1. If   I   need - ed   some -
2., 4. *See additional lyrics*

- one   to ___   love,   you're the   one ___   that   I'd ___   be   think - ing   of. ___

Bridge

If I need - ed some - one. Had you come some oth - er day, then

it might not have been like this. But you see now I'm too much in love.

Verse

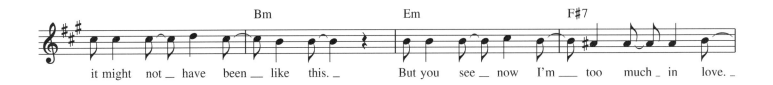

3., 5. Carve your num - ber on my wall and may - be you will get

To Coda

a call from me. If I need - ed some - one.

Interlude

Ah. Ah. Ah.

D.S. al Coda
(no repeat)

Ah.

 Coda

Ah. Ah.

Additional Lyrics

2., 4. If I had some more time to spend,
Then I guess I'd be with you, my friend,
If I needed someone.

The Long and Winding Road

Words and Music by John Lennon and Paul McCartney

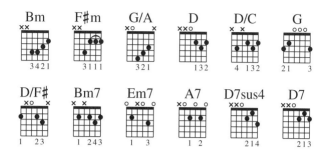

Strum Pattern: 3, 4
Pick Pattern: 1, 3

Verse
Slowly

1. The long and wind-ing road ___ that ___ leads ___ to your door ___
2. *See additional lyrics*

will nev-er dis-ap-pear. I've seen that road be - fore. ___

It al-ways leads ___ me here. Lead me to your ___ door. 2. The way.

Bridge

Man-y times ___ I've been a-lone ___ and man-y times I've cried. ___ An-y-way ___ you'll nev-er know ___ the

Verse

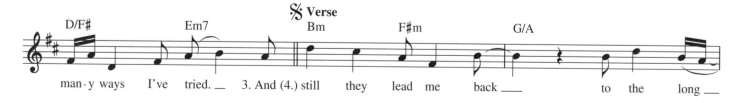

man-y ways I've tried. ___ 3. And (4.) still they lead me back ___ to the long ___

___ wind-ing road. ___ You left me stand - ing here

a long, long time a-go. _____

Don't { leave / keep } me wait - ing here.

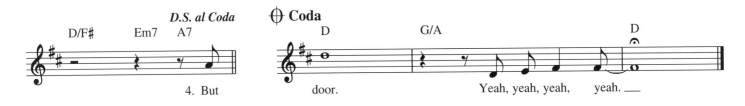

To Coda ⊕

Lead me to your _ door.

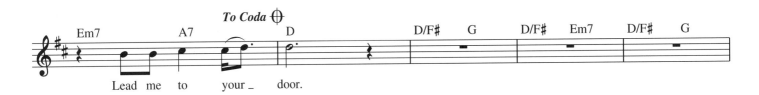

D.S. al Coda   ⊕ **Coda**

4. But

door.

Yeah, yeah, yeah, yeah. _____

Additional Lyrics

2. The wild and windy night
That the rain washed away
Has left a pool of tears
Crying for the day.
Why leave me standing here?
Let me know the way.

Money
(That's What I Want)

Words and Music by Berry Gordy and Janie Bradford

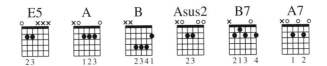

Strum Pattern: 2
Pick Pattern: 4

Intro
Moderate Rock

Verse

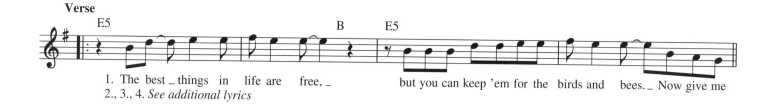

1. The best _ things in life are free, _ but you can keep 'em for the birds and bees. _ Now give me
2., 3., 4. *See additional lyrics*

Chorus

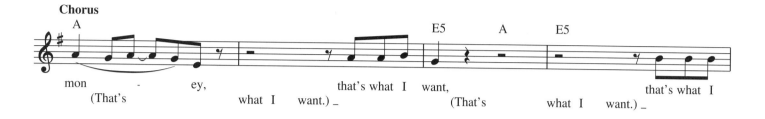

mon - ey, that's what I want, that's what I
(That's what I want.) _ (That's what I want.) _

To Coda ⊕ |1., 2. |3.
D.C. al Coda

want, _____ yeah, _____ that's what I want. _
(That's what I want.) _

⊕ **Coda**
Verse

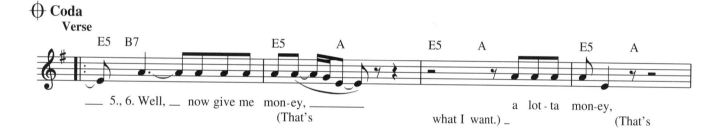

_ 5., 6. Well, _ now give me mon-ey, _____ a lot-ta mon-ey, (That's
(That's what I want.) _

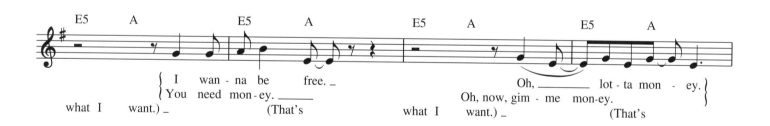

{ I wan - na be free. _ Oh, _____ lot-ta mon - ey. }
{ You need mon-ey. _____ Oh, now, gim - me mon-ey. }
what I want.) _ (That's what I want.) _ (That's

what I want.) _ That's what I want, _____ yeah, _____ that's what I want. ___
(That's what I want.) _

Additional Lyrics

2. Your lovin' give me a thrill,
   But your lovin' don't pay my bills.

3., 4. Money don't get ev'rything it's true,
   What it don't get I can't use.

In My Life

Words and Music by John Lennon and Paul McCartney

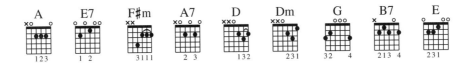

Strum Pattern: 6
Pick Pattern: 5

Intro
Moderately

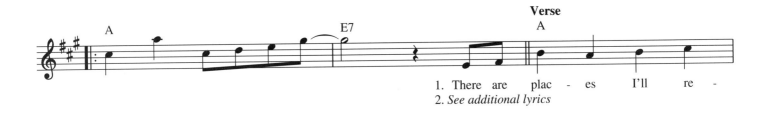
1. There are plac - es I'll re -
2. *See additional lyrics*

mem - ber all my life, _____ though some have changed. _ Some for -

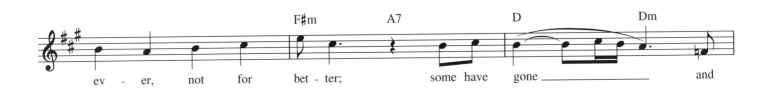
ev - er, not for bet - ter; some have gone _____ and

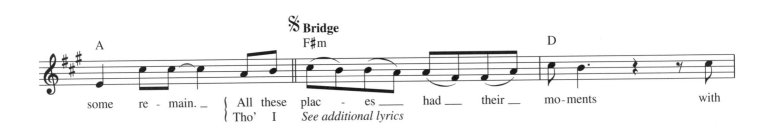
some re - main. _ { All these plac - es _____ had _ their _ mo - ments with
{ Tho' I *See additional lyrics*

lov - ers and friends _ I still can re - call. _ Some are dead _ and _ some _ are _

To Coda ⊕

liv - ing, in my _____ life I've loved them all. _

Interlude

D.S. al Coda
(2nd lyrics)

Tho' I

⊕ **Coda**

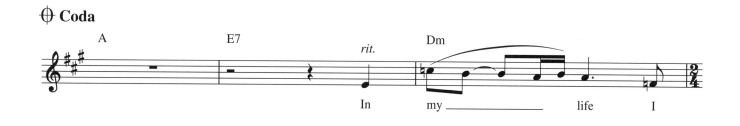

In my _____ life I

A tempo

love you more.

Additional Lyrics

2. But of all these friends and lovers,
   There is no one compares with you.
   And these mem'ries lose their meaning
   When I think of love as something new.

Bridge Tho' I know I'll never lose affection
   For people and things that went before.
   I know I'll often stop and think about them,
   In my life I'll love you more.

Julia

Words and Music by John Lennon and Paul McCartney

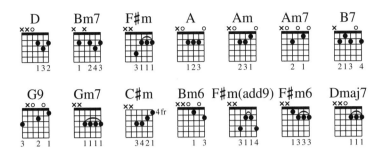

Strum Pattern: 3, 4
Pick Pattern: 1, 3

Moderately slow

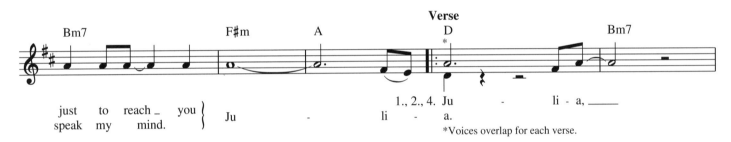

Half of what I say is mean-ing - less. But I say it
When I can-not sing my heart I can on - ly ___

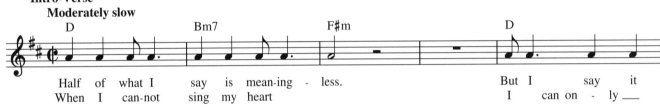

just to reach ___ you } Ju - li - a, ___
speak my mind. 1., 2., 4. Ju - li - a.

Voices overlap for each verse.

To Coda ⊕

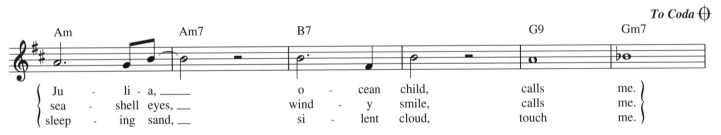

{ Ju - li - a, ___ o - cean child, calls me.
sea - shell eyes, ___ wind - y smile, calls me. }
sleep - ing sand, ___ si - lent cloud, touch me.

So I sing a song ___ of love, ___ Ju - li - a

2.

- li - a.

Bridge

Her hair of float - ing sky is

shim - mer - ing, glim - mer - ing, in the

Verse

sun. _____ 3. Ju - li - a. _____ Ju - li - a, __

___ morn - ing moon touch me. So I sing a song _

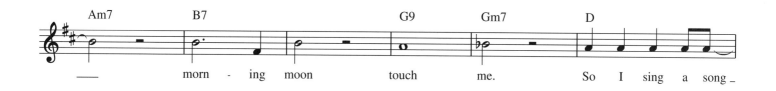

D.C. al Coda

___ of love, _ Ju - li - a.

Coda

So I sing a song __ of love, _ Ju - li - a,

mm, _____ calls

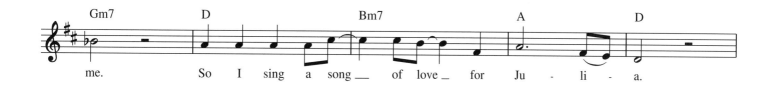

me. So I sing a song __ of love _ for Ju - li - a.

Ju - li - a, Ju - li - a.

Lady Madonna

Words and Music by John Lennon and Paul McCartney

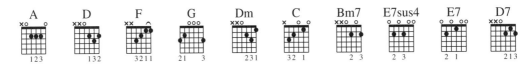

Strum Pattern: 1
Pick Pattern: 1

Verse
Moderate Rock

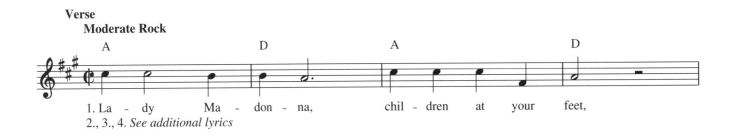

1. La - dy Ma - don - na, chil - dren at your feet,
2., 3., 4. *See additional lyrics*

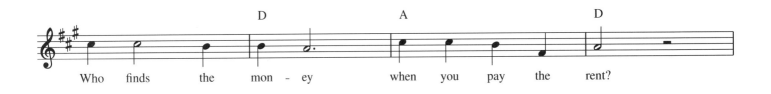

won - der how you man - age to make ___ ends meet? ___

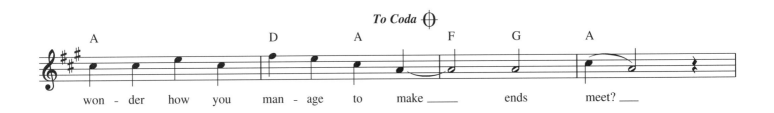

Who finds the mon - ey when you pay the rent?

Did you think that mon - ey was heav - en sent? ___

Bridge

Fri - day night ar - rives with - out a suit - case.

Sun - day morn - ing creep - ing like a nun. _____

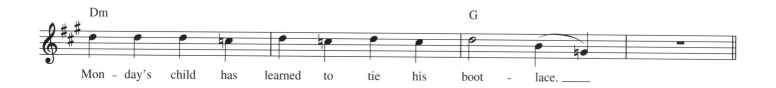

Mon - day's child has learned to tie his boot - lace. _____

Chorus

1., 2.   3.   *D.C. al Coda*

See how they run. _____   run. _____

✛ **Coda**

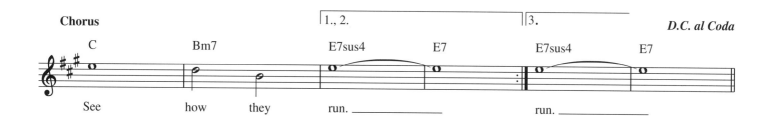

_____   ends   meet. _____

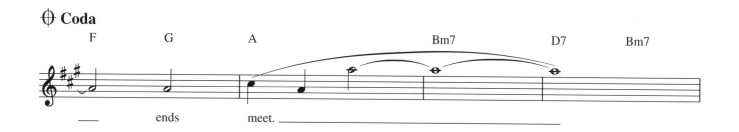

Additional Lyrics

2. Lady Madonna, baby at your breast,
   Wonder how you manage to feed the rest?
   (Instrumental to Chorus)

3. Lady Madonna, lying on the bed,
   Listen to the music playing in your head.
   (Instrumental to Bridge)

Bridge Tuesday afternoon is never ending;
          Wedn'sday morning papers didn't come.
          Thursday night your stockings needed mending.
          See how they run.

4. Lady Madonna, children at your feet,
   Wonder how you manage to make ends meet?

Let It Be

Words and Music by John Lennon and Paul McCartney

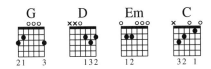

Strum Pattern: 3
Pick Pattern: 4

Verse
Slowly

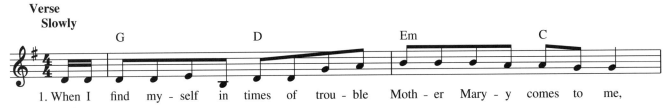

1. When I find my-self in times of trou-ble Moth-er Mar-y-y comes to me,

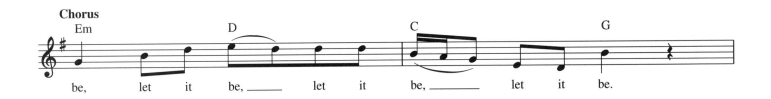

speak-ing words of wis-dom, let it be. ___ And in my hour of dark-ness she is

stand-ing right in front of me, speak-ing words of wis-dom, let it be. ___ Let it

Chorus

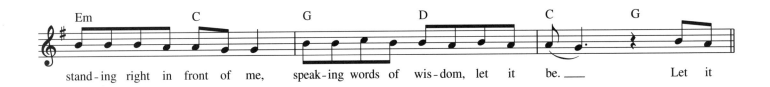

be, let it be, ___ let it be, ___ let it be.

Whis-per words of wis-dom, let it be. ___ 2. And

Verse

when the brok-en-heart-ed peo-ple liv-ing in the world a-gree,
3. See additional lyrics

there will be an an-swer, let it be. ___ For though they may be part-ed there is

still a chance that they will see. There will be an an-swer, let it be. ___ Let it

Chorus

be, let it be, ___ let it be, ___ let it be. ___ There will be an an-swer, let it

be. ___ Let it be, let it be, ___ let it be, ___ let it be.

Interlude

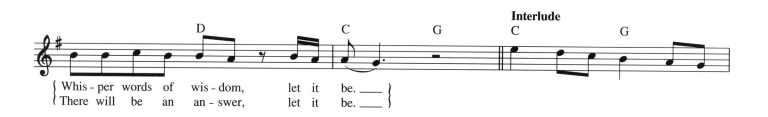

{ Whis-per words of wis-dom, let it be. ___ }
{ There will be an an-swer, let it be. ___ }

Fine   *D.S. al Fine*

3. And

Additional Lyrics

3. And when the night is cloudy, there is still a light that shines on me,
   Shine until tomorrow, let it be.
   I wake up to the sound of music, Mother Mary comes to me,
   Speaking words of wisdom, let it be.

Love Me Do

Words and Music by John Lennon and Paul McCartney

Norwegian Wood
(This Bird Has Flown)

Words and Music by John Lennon and Paul McCartney

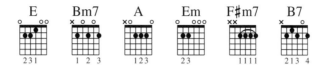

Strum Pattern: 9
Pick Pattern: 7

Moderately

Verse

1. I once had a girl, or should I say she once had me.
3. *Instrumental*

She showed me her room, is-n't it good Nor-we-gian wood? She

Bridge

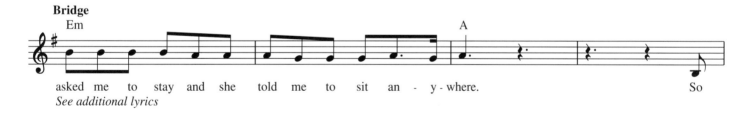

asked me to stay and she told me to sit an-y-where.
See additional lyrics
So

I looked a-round and I no-ticed there was-n't a chair.

Verse

2. I sat on a rug, bid-ing my time, drink-ing her wine.
4. *See additional lyrics*

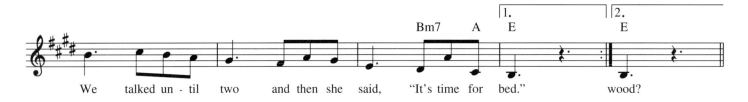

We talked un-til two and then she said, "It's time for bed." wood?

Outro

Additional Lyrics

Bridge She told me she worked in the morning and started to laugh.
I told her I didn't and crawled off to sleep in the bath.

4. And when I awoke I was alone, this bird had flown.
So I lit a fire, isn't it good Norwegian wood?

Nowhere Man

Words and Music by John Lennon and Paul McCartney

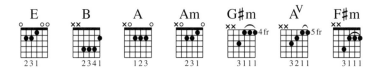

Strum Pattern: 6
Pick Pattern: 4

Intro-Verse
Moderately

He's a real no-where _ man, sit-ting in __ his no-where _ land,

mak-ing all __ his no-where plans for no-bod-y.

% Verse

1. Does-n't have _ a point of view, _ knows not where he's go-ing to. _ Is-n't he _ a bit _
2., 3. *See additional lyrics*

Additional Lyrics

2. He's as blind as he can be,
   Just sees what he wants to see.
   Nowhere man can you see me at all?

Bridge 2. Nowhere man, don't worry.
   Take your time, don't hurry.
   Leave it all till somebody else lends you a hand.

3. Doesn't have a point of view,
   Knows not where he's going to.
   Isn't he a bit like you and me?

Lovely Rita

Words and Music by John Lennon and Paul McCartney

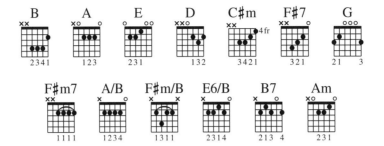

Strum Pattern: 2
Pick Pattern: 4

Intro-Chorus
Moderately

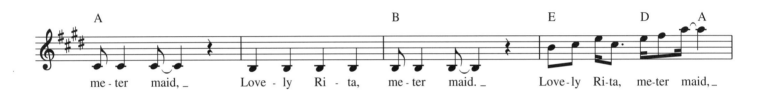

Ah. Love-ly Rita,

me-ter maid, _ Love-ly Ri-ta, me-ter maid. _ Love-ly Rita, me-ter maid, _

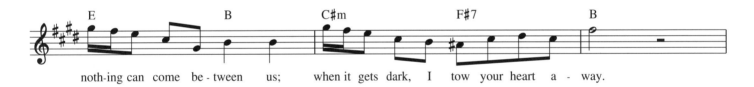

noth-ing can come be - tween us; when it gets dark, I tow your heart a - way.

Verse

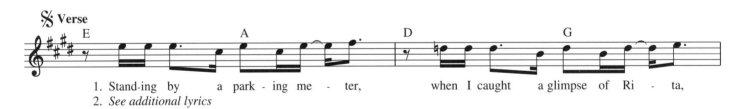

1. Stand-ing by a park - ing me - ter, when I caught a glimpse of Ri-ta,
2. *See additional lyrics*

fill-ing in a tick - et in her lit - tle white book. In a cap she looked much old - er,

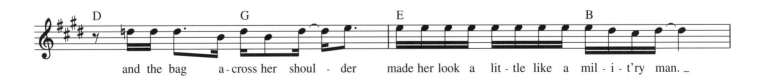

and the bag a-cross her shoul - der made her look a lit - tle like a mil - i - t'ry man. _

Additional Lyrics

2. Took her out and tried to win her,
Had a laugh, and over dinner
Told her I would really like to see her again.
Got the bill and Rita paid it,
Took her home, I nearly made it,
Sitting on the sofa with a sister or two.
Oh, Lovely Rita, meter maid,
Where would I be without you?
Give us a wink and make me think of you.

Lucy in the Sky With Diamonds

Words and Music by John Lennon and Paul McCartney

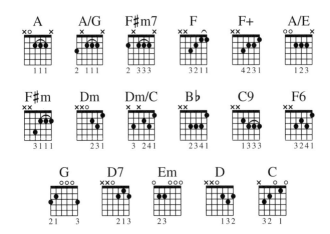

*Strum Pattern: 8
*Pick Pattern: 8

Intro
Moderately

*Use Pattern 4 for ¾ meas.

1. Pic - ture your -
2., 3. *See additional lyrics*

self in a boat on a riv - er with tan - ger - ine ___ trees and mar - ma - lade ___

skies. Some - bod - y calls you, you an - swer quite slow - ly, a

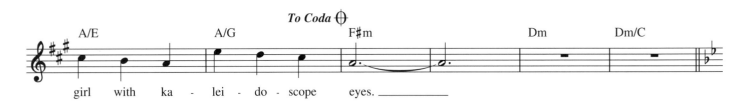

girl with ka - lei - do - scope eyes. ___

Pre-Chorus

Cel - lo - phane flow - ers of yel - low and green tow - er - ing ___ o - ver your
See additional lyrics

head. _____ Look for the girl with the sun in her eyes and she's

Moderately slow (♩. = ♩)
Chorus

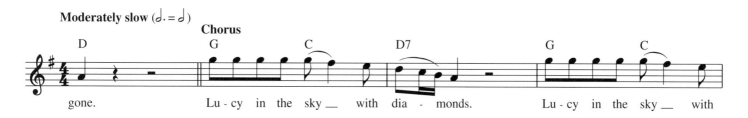

gone. Lu - cy in the sky __ with dia - monds. Lu - cy in the sky __ with

dia - monds, Lu - cy in the sky __ with dia - monds. Ah. Ah.

D.S. al Coda

⊕ **Coda**

Outro-Chorus

eyes. _____ Lu - cy in the sky ___ with

dia - monds. Lu - cy in the sky ___ with dia - monds.

Repeat and fade

Lu - cy in the sky ___ with dia - monds. Ah. _____

Additional Lyrics

2. Follow her down to a bridge by a fountain,
   Where rocking horse people eat marshmallow pies.
   Ev'ryone smiles as you drift past the flowers
   That grow so incredibly high.

Pre-Chorus Newspaper taxis appear on the shore
   Waiting to take you away.
   Climb in the back with your
   Head in the clouds and you're gone.

3. Picture yourself on a train in a station
   With plasticine porters with looking glass ties.
   Suddenly someone is there at the turnstile,
   The girl with kaleidoscope eyes.

Magical Mystery Tour

Words and Music by John Lennon and Paul McCartney

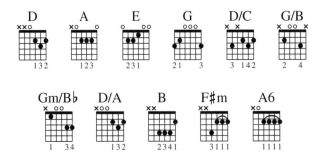

*Strum Pattern: 6
*Pick Pattern: 4

Intro
Moderately

Spoken: Roll up, roll up for the Magical Mystery Tour. Step right this way.

*Use Pattern 9 for ⅜ meas.

Verse

1., 3. Roll up, _____ roll up __ for the mys - ter - y tour. _ Roll up, _____

2. *See additional lyrics*

__ roll up __ for the mys - ter - y tour. _ Roll up __ and that's an

in - vi - ta - tion. Roll up ____ for the mys - ter - y tour. _

To Coda ⊕

Roll up, ___ to make a res - er - va - tion. Roll up __ for the mys -

Chorus

- ter - y tour. The Mag - i - cal Mys - ter - y Tour is

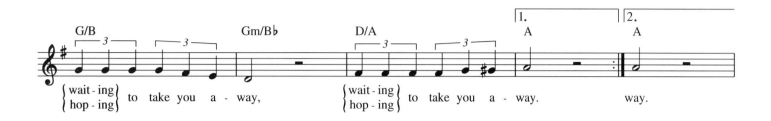

{ wait - ing / hop - ing } to take you a - way, { wait - ing / hop - ing } to take you a - way. way.

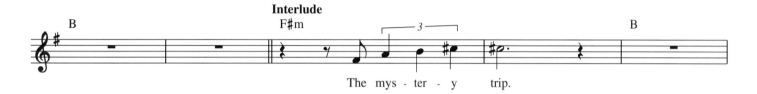

Interlude

The mys - ter - y trip.

D.S. al Coda

The mys - ter - y trip.

⊕ **Coda**

Outro-Chorus

- ter - y tour. The Mag - i - cal Mys - ter - y Tour is

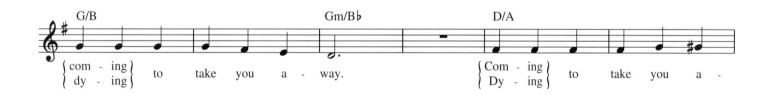

{ com - ing / dy - ing } to take you a - way. { Com - ing / Dy - ing } to take you a -

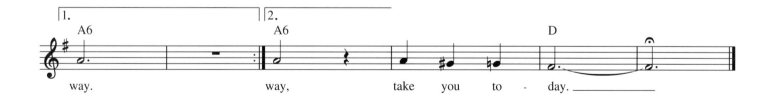

way. way, take you to - day.

Additional Lyrics

2. Roll up, roll up for the mystery tour.
Roll up, roll up for the mystery tour.
Roll up, we've got ev'rything you need.
Roll up for the mystery tour.
Roll up, satisfaction guaranteed.
Roll up for the mystery tour.

Michelle

Words and Music by John Lennon and Paul McCartney

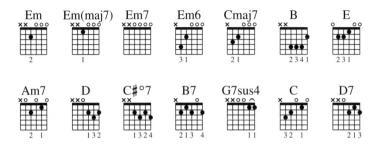

Strum Pattern: 2
Pick Pattern: 4

Intro

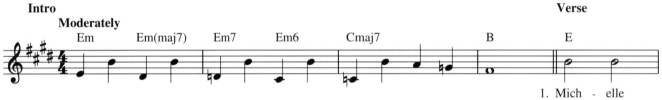

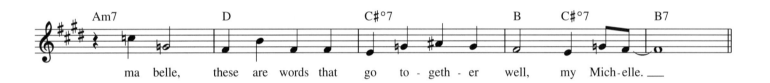

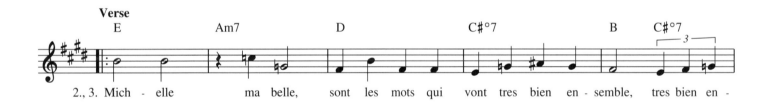

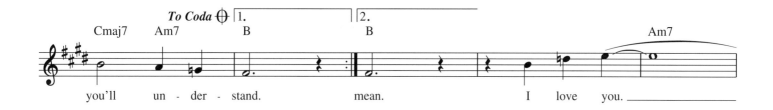

you'll un - der - stand. mean. I love you. _____

D.S. al Coda

3. I

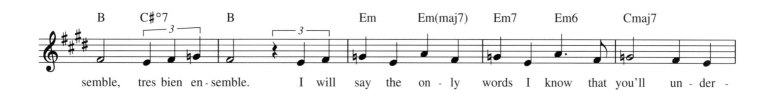

⊕ **Coda**

stand. 4. Mich - elle ma belle, sont les mots qui vont tres bien en -

semble, tres bien en - semble. I will say the on - ly words I know that you'll un - der -

Outro

stand, my Mich - elle. _____

Repeat and fade

Additional Lyrics

Bridge 2. I need you, I need you, I need you,
I need to make you see,
Oh, what you mean to me.
Until I do I'm hoping you will know what I mean.

Bridge 3. I want you, I want you, I want you,
I think you know by now
I'll get to you somehow.
Until I do I'm telling you so you'll understand.

Mother Nature's Son

Words and Music by John Lennon and Paul McCartney

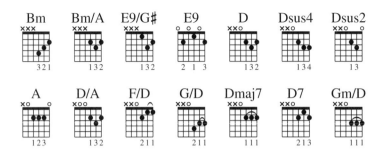

Strum Pattern: 2
Pick Pattern: 4

Intro
Slowly

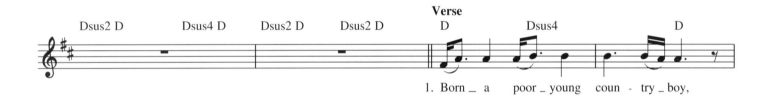

1. Born _ a poor _ young coun - try _ boy,

Moth - er Na - ture's _ son. All day _ long _ I'm _

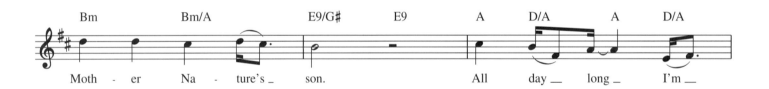

sit - ting sing - ing songs _ for ev - 'ry - one. ___

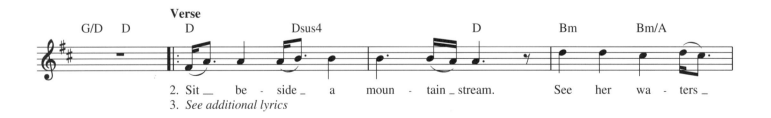

2. Sit _ be - side _ a moun - tain _ stream. See her wa - ters _
3. *See additional lyrics*

rise. Lis - ten _ to _ the _ pret-ty sound _ of mu - sic as she flies. _

Bridge

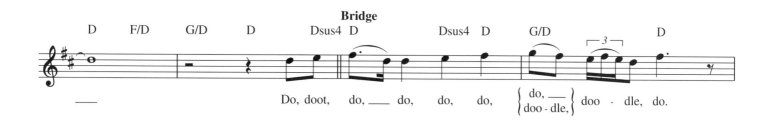

_ Do, doot, do, _ do, do, do, { do, _ / doo - dle, } doo - dle, do.

Do, _ do, do, do, do, _ doo - dle, do, mm, do, _ do, _ / mm, do, do, do, do, do, _

*Use Pattern 10

1.   2.   **Verse**

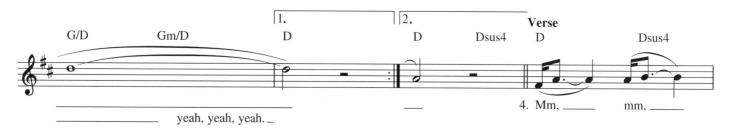

_ yeah, yeah, yeah. _   _   4. Mm, _ mm, _

mm, mm, _ mm, oo, _ oo. _

Mm, _ mm, _ mm, _ do - wah, _

_ oo, _ ah, _ mm. Mo-ther Na - ture's _ son.

Additional Lyrics

3. Find me in my field of grass,
Mother Nature's son.
Swaying daisies sing a lazy
Song beneath the sun.

Ob-La-Di, Ob-La-Da

Words and Music by John Lennon and Paul McCartney

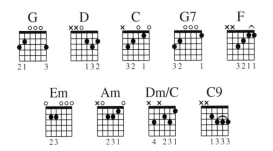

Strum Pattern: 4
Pick Pattern: 4

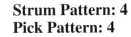

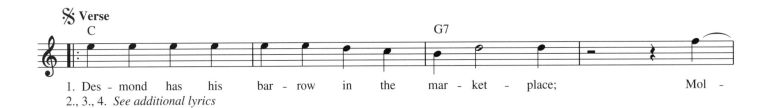

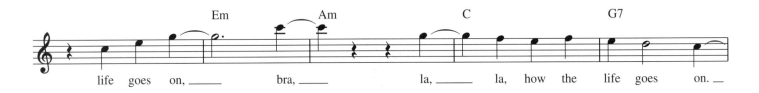

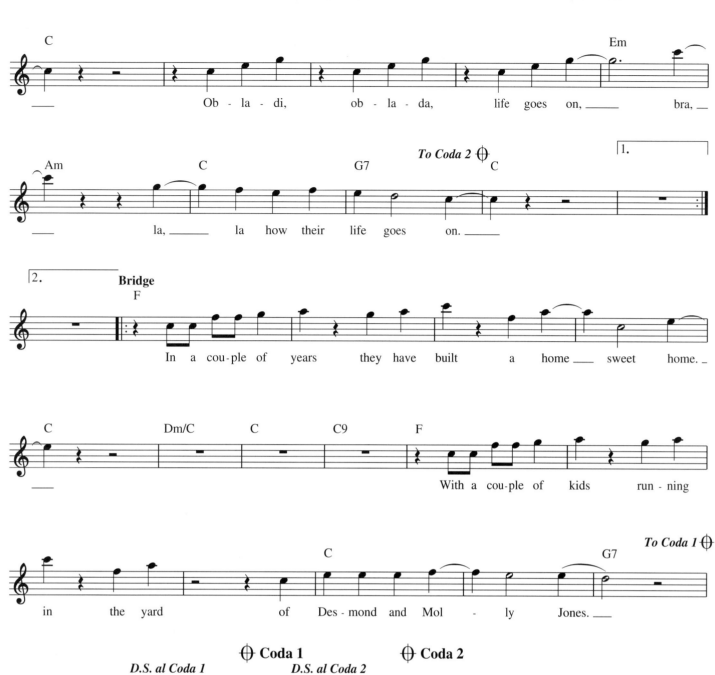

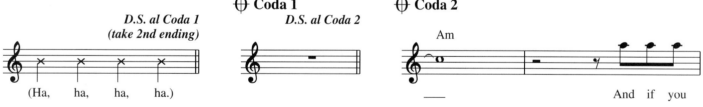

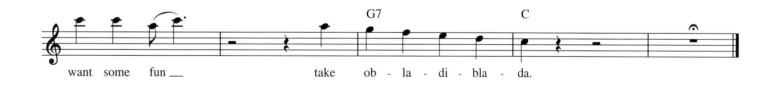

Additional Lyrics

2. Desmond takes a trolley to the jeweler's store,
Buys a twenty carat golden ring. (Ring.)
Takes it back to Molly waiting at the door
And as he gives it to her she begins to sing:

3. Happy ever after in the marketplace;
Desmond lets the children lend a hand.
Molly stays at home and does her pretty face
And in the evening she still sings it with the band.

4. Happy ever after in the marketplace;
Molly lets the children lend a hand.
Desmond stays at home and does his pretty face.
And in the evening she's a singer with the band.

Octopus's Garden

Words and Music by Richard Starkey

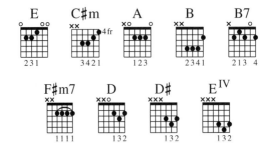

Strum Pattern: 3, 4
Pick Pattern: 1, 3

Intro

Moderately bright

Verse

1. I'd like to be ___ un - der the sea ___ in an oct - o - pus's gar -
3. *See additional lyrics*

- den in the shade. He'd let us in; ___

knows where we've been, ___ in his oct - o - pus's gar - den in the shade.

Bridge

I'd ask my friends to come and see ___ an oct - o -
See additional lyrics

read my book? It took me years to write, _ will you take a look? It's

Verse

pus - 's gar-den with me. _____ 2., 4. I'd like to be ___

un-der the sea ___ in an oct-o-pus-'s gar - den in the shade. _

|1. |2. **Interlude** |1.

|2.

Verse

5. We would shout _ and swim a - bout ___ the cor-al _____ that

lies be-neath the waves. _ Oh, what joy ___ for

ev-'ry girl and boy ___ know-ing ___ they're hap-py and they're safe.

Bridge

We would be so hap-py ___ you and me; ___ no one there to

Outro-Verse

tell us what to do. ___ I'd like to be ___

un - der the sea ___ in an oct - o - pus - 's gar - den with you, _

___ in an oct - o - pus - 's gar - den with you, ___

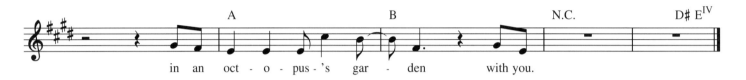

in an oct - o - pus - 's gar - den with you.

Additional Lyrics

3. We would be warm below the storm
   In our little hideaway beneath the waves,
   Resting our head on the sea bed
   In an octopus's garden near a cave.

Bridge We would sing and dance around
   Because we know we can't be found.

Paperback Writer

Words and Music by John Lennon and Paul McCartney

Strum Pattern: 2
Pick Pattern: 4

Intro
Bright Rock

Pa - per-back writ - er. Pa - per-back writ - er.

1. Dear _ Sir or Mad-am, will you
3. *See additional lyrics*

read   my   book?   It   took   me   years   to   write, ___   will   you   take   a   look?   It's

based   on   a   nov - el   by   a   man   named   Lear   and   I   need   a   job ___   so   I

C   G7

want   to   be   a   pa - per - back   writ - er, _____   pa - per - back   writ - er. _____

Verse
G7

___   2. It's   the   dirt - y   sto - ry   of   a   dirt - y   man __   and   his   cling - ing   wife __   does-n't
4. *See additional lyrics*

un - der-stand.   His   son   is   work - ing   for   the   Dai - ly   Mail. __   It's   a   stead - y   job, __   but   he

C   G7   *2nd time, D.C. al Coda*

wants   to   be   a   pa - per-back   writ - er, _____   pa - per - back   writ - er. _____

✛ **Coda**   **Outro**   *Repeat and fade*
                              G7

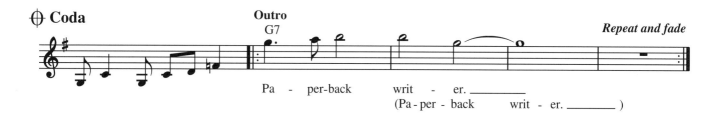

Pa - per-back   writ - er. _____
(Pa - per - back   writ - er. _____)

Additional Lyrics

3. It's a thousand pages, give or take a few;
   I'll be writing more in a week or two.
   I can make it longer if you like the style,
   I can change it 'round, and I want to be a paperback writer,
   Paperback writer.

4. If you really like it you can have the rights;
   It could make a million for you overnight.
   If you must return it you can send it here,
   But I need a break and I want to be a paperback writer,
   Paperback writer.

Oh! Darling

Words and Music by John Lennon and Paul McCartney

Strum Pattern: 1, 3
Pick Pattern: 2, 4

Slowly

Verse

1. Oh __ dar-ling, please be-lieve me, _____ I'll nev-er do you no
2. *See additional lyrics*

harm. _ Be - lieve me when I tell you, I'll nev-er do you no

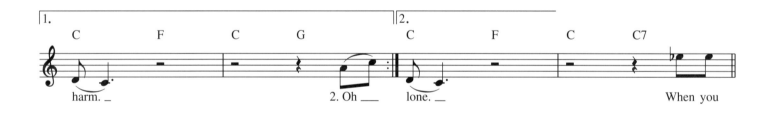

harm. _   2. Oh __ lone. _   When you

Chorus

told me you did-n't need me an - y - more, well you know I near - ly broke down and

cried. _____ When you told me you did-n't need me an - y - more, well you

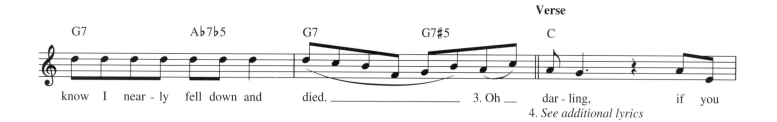

know I near-ly fell down and died. _____ 3. Oh __ dar-ling, if you
4. *See additional lyrics*

leave me, _____ I'll nev-er make it a lone. _____ Be -

lieve me when I tell you, I'll nev-er do you no harm. _ *Spoken: Believe me, darling.* When you

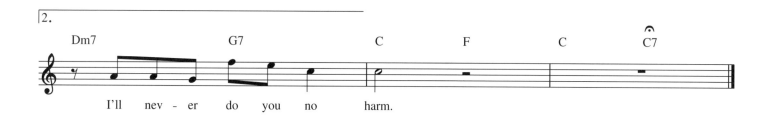

I'll nev-er do you no harm.

Additional Lyrics

2. Oh darling, if you leave me,
I'll never make it alone.
Believe me when I beg you,
Don't ever leave me alone.

4. Oh, darling, please believe me,
I'll never let you down.
Believe me when I tell you,
I'll never do you no harm.

Old Brown Shoe

Words and Music by George Harrison

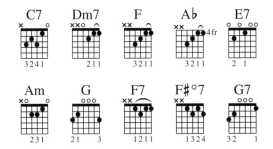

Strum Pattern: 2
Pick Pattern: 4

1. I want a

love that's right, _ right _ is on-ly half of what's wrong. _ I want a

2., 4. *See additional lyrics*
3. *Instrumental*

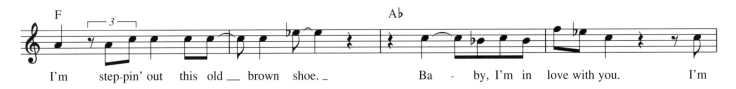

short-haired girl _ who some-times wears it twice as long. _ Now

I'm step-pin' out this old _ brown shoe. _ Ba - by, I'm in love with you. I'm

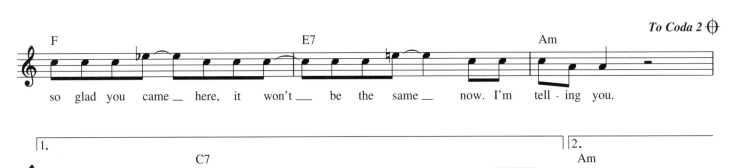

so glad you came _ here, it won't _ be the same _ now. I'm tell - ing you.

1.
C7

2.
Am

2. Though you

Bridge

If I grow up I'll ___ be a sing - er, wearing rings on ev - 'ry fin - ger,
See additional lyrics

not wor - ry - ing what they ___ or you'll ___ say. I'll live and love ___ and

may - be some - day, who knows, ba - by? You may com - fort me. _____

To Coda 1

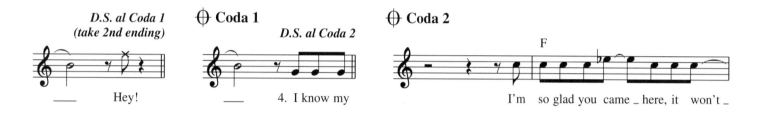

D.S. al Coda 1
(take 2nd ending)

___ Hey!

Coda 1

D.S. al Coda 2

___ 4. I know my

Coda 2

I'm so glad you came ___ here, it won't ___

___ be the same ___ now, when I'm with you.

Outro

Repeat and fade

Additional Lyrics

2. Though you picked me up
   From where some try to drag me down.
   And when I see your smile
   Replacing ev'ry thoughtless frown.
   Got me escaping from this zoo.
   Baby, I'm in love with you.
   I'm so glad you came here,
   It won't be the same now, when I'm with you.

Bridge I may appear to be imperfect,
   My love is something you can't reject.
   I'm changing faster than the weather,
   If you and me should get together,
   Who knows, baby? You may comfort me.

4. I know my love is yours;
   To miss that love is something I'd hate.
   I'll make an early start,
   I'm making sure that I'm not late.
   For your sweet top lip I'm in the queue.
   Baby, I'm in love with you.
   I'm so glad you came here,
   It won't be the same now, when I'm with you.

Penny Lane

Words and Music by John Lennon and Paul McCartney

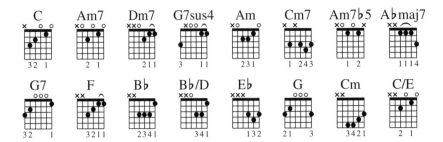

Strum Pattern: 4
Pick Pattern: 4

𝄋 **Verse**

Moderately

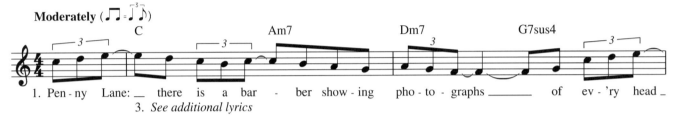

1. Pen-ny Lane: __ there is a bar - ber show-ing pho-to-graphs _____ of ev-'ry head _
3. *See additional lyrics*

__ he's had the plea-sure to know, __ and all the peo-ple that come and go _

__ stop and say __ hel-lo.   On the cor-ner is a bank-er with a

mo-tor-car; __ the lit-tle chil - dren laugh at him be-hind his back.   And the

bank-er nev-er wears a mac __ in the pour-ing rain,   ve-ry strange! _ Pen-ny Lane _

Chorus

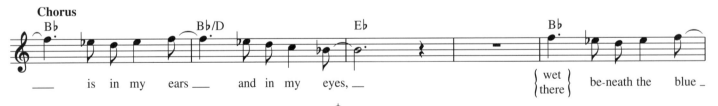

__ is in my ears __ and in my eyes, __   { wet / there } be-neath the blue _

To Coda ✠   **Verse**

__ sub-ur-ban skies __ I sit. 2., 4. And mean-while back in Pen-ny Lane _ there is a fire-man with an

hour _ glass, _ and in his pock - et is a por - trait of the Queen. _ He likes to

keep his fi - re en - gine clean; _ it's a clean _ ma-chine!

Interlude

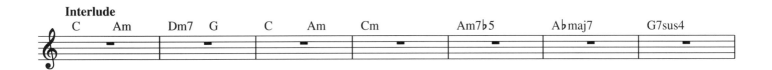

Chorus

Pen-ny Lane _ is in my ears ___ and in my eyes. _

D.S. al Coda

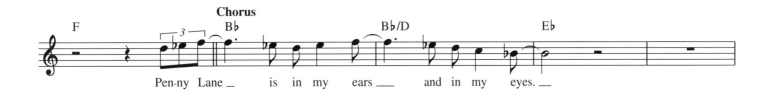

Full of fish ___ and fin - ger pies ___ in sum - mer. 3. Mean - while back be - hind the

⊕ **Coda**

mean - while back... Pen-ny Lane _ is in my ears ___ and in my eyes. _

There be-neath the blue _ sub-ur-ban skies. _ Pen-ny Lane. _____

Additional Lyrics

3. Meanwhile back behind the shelter in the middle of the roundabout,
The pretty nurse is selling poppies from a tray.
And though she feels as if she's in a play
She is anyway.
Penny Lane: The barber shaves another customer,
We see the banker sitting, waiting for a trim.
And then the fireman rushes in
From the pouring rain, very strange!

Please Please Me

Words and Music by John Lennon and Paul McCartney

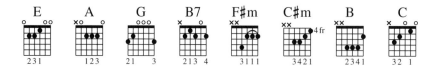

Strum Pattern: 1
Pick Pattern: 2

1., 3. Last night I said these words to my _____ girl,
2. *See additional lyrics*

I know {you / I} nev-er e-ven try, _____ girl.

Come on, (Come on.) _ come on. (Come on.) _ Come on, (Come on.) _ come

on. (Come on.) _ Please, please me, whoa, yeah, like I please you.

Bridge

I don't want to sound com-plain-ing but you know there's al-ways rain in my _____ heart.

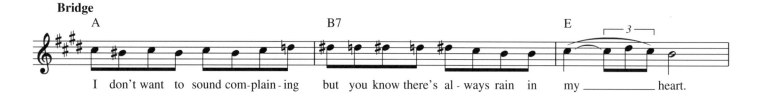

(In _ my heart.) I do all the pleas-ing with you, it's so hard to rea-son with

you, whoa, yeah, why do you make me blue?

Coda **Outro**

yeah, like I please you, whoa, yeah, like I please you. _____

Additional Lyrics

2. You don't need me to show the way love,
Why do I always have to say, love.
Come on, (Come on.) come on. (Come on.)
Come on, (Come on.) come on. (Come on.)
Please, please me, whoa, yeah,
Like I please you.

P.S. I Love You

Words and Music by John Lennon and Paul McCartney

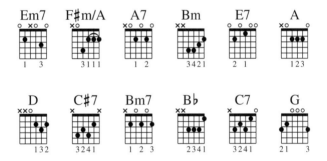

Strum Pattern: 2
Pick Pattern: 4

Intro
Moderate Rock

1. As I write this

let - ter, send my love to you. Re - mem - ber that I'll al - ways

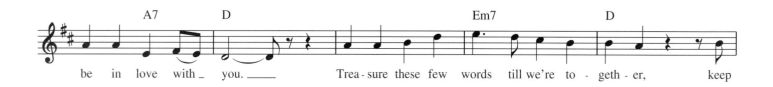

be in love with _ you. _____ Trea - sure these few words till we're to - geth - er, keep

all my love for - ev - er, P. S. I love you, _____ you, _ you, _

§ Verse

you. _____ 2., 4. I'll be com - ing home a - gain to you love and
3. *See additional lyrics*

To Coda ⊕

till the day I do love, P. S. I love you, _____ you, _ you, _ you. _____

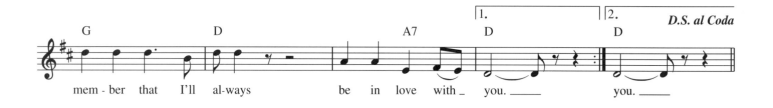

_ As I write this let - ter send my love to you, re -

D.S. al Coda

mem - ber that I'll al-ways be in love with _ you. _____ you. _____

⊕ **Coda**

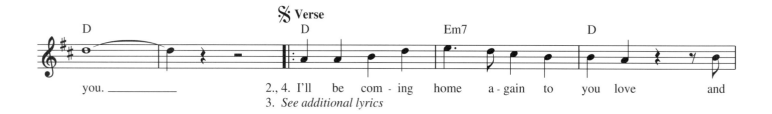

you, _____ you, _ you, _ you, _____ I love you. _____

Additional Lyrics

3. Treasure these few words till we're together,
   Keep all my love forever.
   P.S. I love you, you, you, you.
   As I write this letter, oh,
   Send my love to you, you know I want you to
   Remember that I'll always, yeah, be in love with you.

Polythene Pam

Words and Music by John Lennon and Paul McCartney

Strum Pattern: 2
Pick Pattern: 4

Intro
Brightly

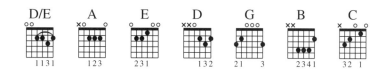

1. Well, you should see Pol - y - thene Pam, ___

___ she's so good - look - ing but she looks like a man. ___ Well, you should

see her in drag, _ dressed in her pol - y - thene bag. _ Yes, you should see Pol - y - thene Pam. _

___ Yeah, yeah, yeah. ___

2. Get a dose of her in jack-boots and kilt. ___ She's kill - er

dill - er when she's dressed to the hilt. ___ She's the kind of a girl ___ that makes the

"News of the World." _ Yes, you could say she was at-tract-ive-ly built. _ Yeah, yeah, yeah. _

Segue to "She Came In Through the Bathroom Window"

Outro

Play 10 times

Real Love

Words and Music by John Lennon

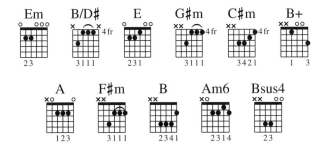

Strum Pattern: 2
Pick Pattern: 4

Intro
Moderately

1. All my lit-tle plans and schemes,_

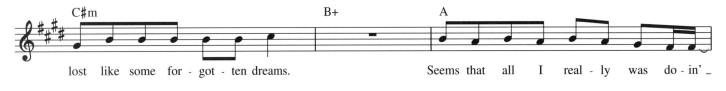

lost like some for-got-ten dreams. Seems that all I real-ly was do-in'_

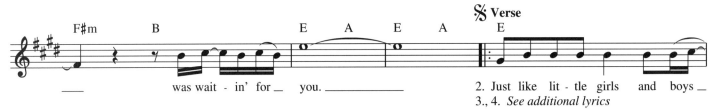

was wait-in' for_ you. _____ 2. Just like lit-tle girls and boys_
3., 4. *See additional lyrics*

play-ing with their lit-tle toys, seems like all we real-ly were do-in'

Pre-Chorus

was wait-in' for_ love. _____ 1., 3. No need to be _ a-lone.
2. No need to be _ a-fraid.

Chorus

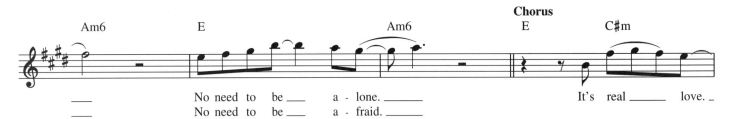

No need to be _ a-lone. _____ It's real _____ love. _
No need to be _ a-fraid. _____

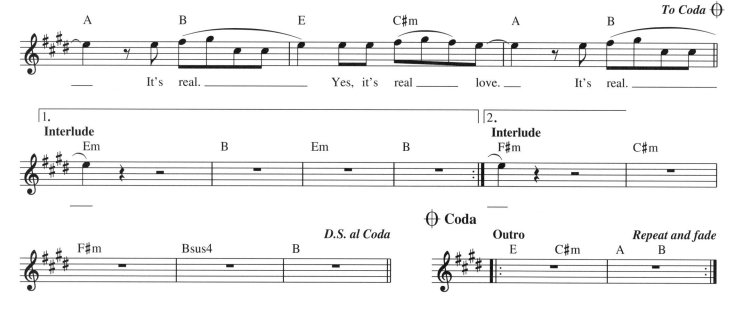

It's real. _____ Yes, it's real _____ love. _____ It's real. _____

Interlude

Interlude

⊕ **Coda**

D.S. al Coda

Outro *Repeat and fade*

Additional Lyrics

3. From this moment on I know
   Exactly where my life will go.
   Seems that all I really was doin'
   Was waitin' for love.

4. Thought I'd been in love before,
   But in my heart I wanted more.
   Seems that all I really was doin'
   Was waitin' for you.

Sexy Sadie

Words and Music by John Lennon and Paul McCartney

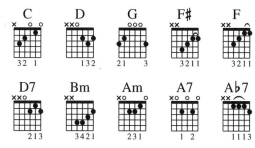

Strum Pattern: 3
Pick Pattern: 3

Intro
Slowly

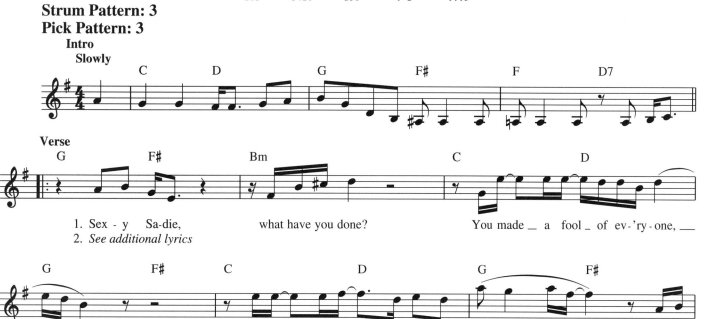

1. Sex - y Sa - die, what have you done? You made _ a fool _ of ev-'ry-one, _
2. *See additional lyrics*

you made _ a fool _ of ev - 'ry - one. _____ Sex-y

Sa-die. Oh, __ what have you done? Sa-die. Oh, __ you broke the rules. __ One sun-ny day, the world was wait - ing for a
See additional lyrics

lov-er; she came a-long to turn __ on ev - 'ry - one. _____ Sex - y Sa -

- die, the great - est of them all. _____ 3. Sex - y Sa-die, how did you know
4. *See additional lyrics*

the world __ was wait - ing just for you, _____ the world __ was wait - ing just for

you? _____ Sex-y Sa - die. Oh, _____ how did you know? Sa - die. Oh, _____ you'll get yours yet. __

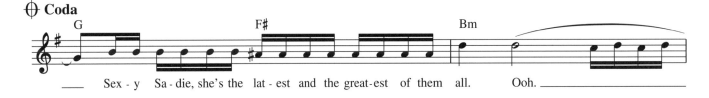

_____ Sex - y Sa - die, she's the lat - est and the great-est of them all. Ooh. _____

Additional Lyrics

2. Sexy Sadie, you broke the rules.
   You laid it down for all to see,
   You laid it down for all to see.
   Sexy Sadie.

4. Sexy Sadie, you'll get yours yet,
   However big you think you are,
   However big you think you are.
   Sexy Sadie.

Bridge Oh, you'll get yours yet.
   You gave her ev'rything you owned
   Just to sit at her table;
   Just a smile would lighten ev'rything.
   Sexy Sadie,
   The latest and the greatest of them all.

Revolution

Words and Music by John Lennon and Paul McCartney

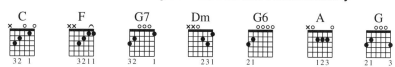

*Strum Pattern: 2
*Pick Pattern: 2

Intro
Moderate Shuffle

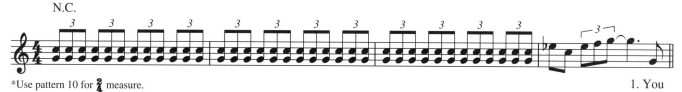

*Use pattern 10 for 2/4 measure.

1. You

Verse

say you want a rev-o - lu - tion, _____ well _____ you know, __ we all want to change the
2., 3. *See additional lyrics*

world. You tell me that it's e-vo - lu - tion, _ well _ you know, _ we all want to change the

world. _____ But when you talk a-bout de-struc-tion, _____ don't you know that you can count me out.

Chorus

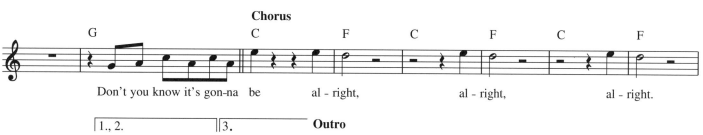

Don't you know it's gon-na be al - right, al - right, al - right.

Outro

2. You Al - right, al - right, al - right, al - right.

Additional Lyrics

2. You say you got a real solution,
   Well you know,
   We'd all love to see the plan.
   You ask me for a contribution,
   Well you know,
   We're all doing what we can.
   But if you want money for people with minds that hate,
   All I can tell you is, "Brother you have to wait."

3. You say you'll change the constitution,
   Well you know,
   We all want to change your head.
   You tell me it's the institution,
   Well you know,
   You better free your mind instead.
   But if you go carrying pictures of Chairman Mao,
   You ain't going to make it with anyone, anyhow.

Rocky Raccoon

Words and Music by John Lennon and Paul McCartney

Strum Pattern: 2
Pick Pattern: 4

Intro
Moderately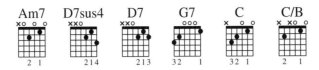

Intro-Verse

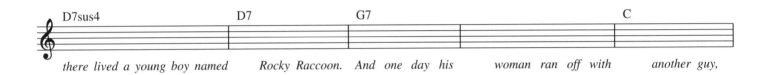

Spoken: Now somewhere in the Black Mountain Hills of Dakota

there lived a young boy named   Rocky Raccoon. And one day his   woman ran off with   another guy,

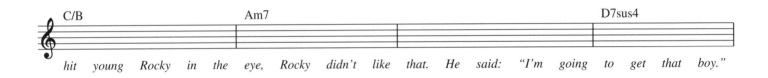

hit   young   Rocky   in   the   eye,   Rocky   didn't   like   that.   He   said: "I'm   going   to   get   that   boy."

So   one   day   he   walked   into   town   and   booked   himself   a   room   in   the   local   saloon.

Verse

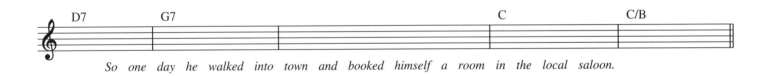

1. Rock - y   Rac - coon ___   checked   in - to   his   room ___   on - ly   to   find _
2. *See additional lyrics*

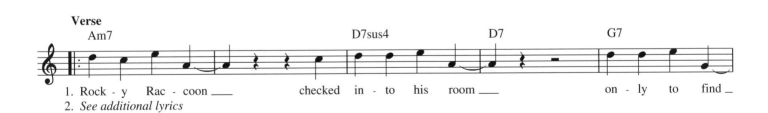

___ Gid - eon's Bi - ble.   Rock - y   had   come ___   e - quipped   with   a   gun _

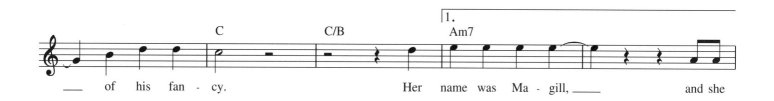

said, "Doc, it's on-ly a scratch, _ and I'll be bet-ter, I'll be bet-ter Doc, as soon _ as I am

a - ble." Now Rock - y Rac - coon, ___ he fell back in his room _

_ on - ly to find ___ Gid - eon's Bi - ble.

Gid - deon checked out ___ and he left it no doubt ___ to help with good Rock -

Outro

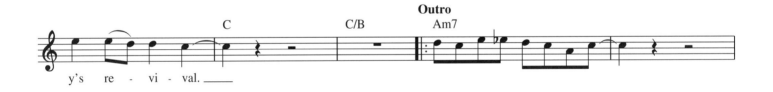

y's re - vi - val. ___

Additional Lyrics

2. Now she and her man who called himself Dan
   Were in the next room at the hoedown.
   Rocky burst in and grinning a grin,
   He said, "Danny boy, this is a showdown."
   But Daniel was hot, he drew first and shot
   And Rocky collapsed in the corner.

She's a Woman

Words and Music by John Lennon and Paul McCartney

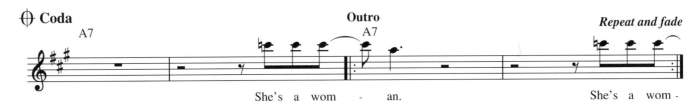

Bridge

D.S. al Coda

She's a wom - an who un - der - stands; _ she's a wom - an who loves her man. _

Coda

Outro

Repeat and fade

She's a wom - an. She's a wom -

Additional Lyrics

2. She don't give boys the eye.
   She hates to see me cry.
   She is happy just to hear me
   Say that I will never leave her;
   She don't give boys the eye.
   She will never make me jealous,
   Gives me all her time as well as lovin',
   Don't ask me why.

Strawberry Fields Forever

Words and Music by John Lennon and Paul McCartney

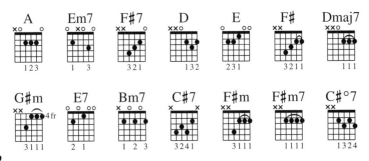

*Strum Pattern: 2
*Pick Pattern: 4

Intro

Slowly

*Use Pattern 10 for 2/4 meas. & Pattern 8 for 4/4 meas.

Chorus

Let me take you down _ 'cause I'm go - in' to _____ Straw - ber - ry Fields.

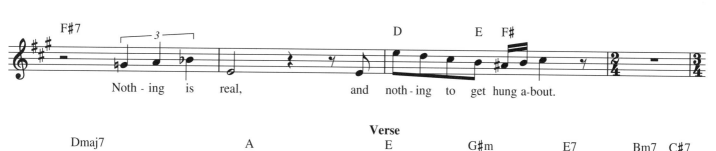

Noth - ing is real, and noth - ing to get hung a - bout.

Verse

Straw-ber - ry Fields _ for - ev - er.
1. Liv - ing is eas - y with eyes closed, _
2., 3. *See additional lyrics*

mis - un - der - stand - ing all you see. _____ It's get - ting hard to be some -

one but it all _ works _ out, it does - n't mat - ter much to me.

Chorus

Let me take you down _ 'cause I'm go - ing to _____ Straw-ber - ry Fields.

Noth - ing is real, and noth - ing to get hung a - bout...

Straw-ber - ry Fields _ for - ev - er. Straw-ber - ry Fields _ for -

ev - er. Straw-ber - ry Fields _ for - ev - er, Straw-ber - ry Fields _ for - ev - er.

Additional Lyrics

2. No one I think is in my tree;
I mean it must be high or low.
That is, you know you can't tune in, but it's alright,
That is, I think it's not too bad.

3. Always know, sometimes think it's me,
But you know I know when it's a dream.
I think a "No" will be a "Yes," but it's all wrong,
That is, I think I disagree.

Sgt. Pepper's Lonely Hearts Club Band

Words and Music by John Lennon and Paul McCartney

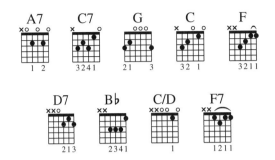

Strum Pattern: 1
Pick Pattern: 2

Intro
Moderately slow

1. It was

Verse

twen-ty years a - go to - day _ Ser-geant Pep-per taught the band to play. _ They've been

2. See additional lyrics

go - ing in and out of style, _ but they're guar-an-teed to raise a smile. _ So

may I in-tro-duce to you _ the act you've known for all these years: _

Interlude

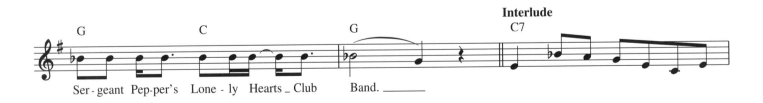

Ser-geant Pep-per's Lone - ly Hearts _ Club Band. _____

We're

Chorus

Ser-geant Pep-per's Lone - ly Hearts _ Club Band. _ { We hope you will en - joy the show. _ / We hope you have en-joyed the show. _ }

Ser-geant Pep-per's Lone - ly Hearts _ Club Band. _ { Sit back and let the eve - ning go. ____ / We're sor - ry but it's time to go. ____ }

Ser - geant Pep-per's Lone - ly, Ser - geant Pep-per's Lone - ly, Ser - geant Pep-per's Lone - ly Hearts _

1.
Bridge

___ Club Band. _ It's won-der - ful to be here, it's cer - tain - ly a thrill. You're

such a love - ly au - di - ence, we'd like to take you home with us, we'd love to take you home. 2. I don't

2.

Ser-geant Pep-per's Lone - ly Hearts _ Club Band, _ we'd like to thank you once a - gain. _

Ser-geant Pep-per's one and on - ly Lone - ly Hearts Club Band, it's get-ting ver - y near the end. _

_ Ser-geant Pep-per's Lone - ly, Ser - geant Pep-per's Lone - ly, Ser - geant Pep-per's Lone - ly Hearts _

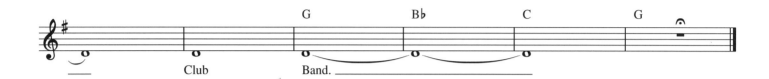

_ Club Band. _

Additional Lyrics

2. I don't really want to stop the show
   But I thought you might like to know
   That the singer's going to sing a song,
   And he wants you all to sing along.
   So let me introduce to you
   The one and only Billy Shears
   And Sergeant Pepper's Lonely Hearts Club Band.

She Came in Through the Bathroom Window

Words and Music by John Lennon and Paul McCartney

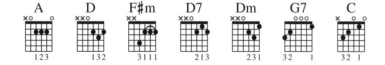

Strum Pattern: 1
Pick Pattern: 2

Intro
Moderately slow

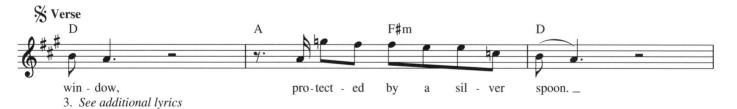

1. She came in through _ the bath-room

 Verse

win - dow, pro-tect - ed by a sil - ver spoon. _

3. *See additional lyrics*

But now she sucks her thumb and wan-ders by the banks of her own la-goon. _

Chorus

Did-n't an-y-bod-y tell ____ her? Did-n't an-y-bod-y see? _

To Coda ⊕

____ Sun-day's on the phone to Mon-day,

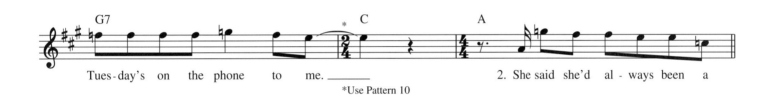

Tues-day's on the phone to me. _____ 2. She said she'd al-ways been a

*Use Pattern 10

Verse

danc-er, she worked in fif-teen clubs a day. ___

D.S. al Coda

And though she thought I knew the an-swer, well, I knew but I could not say. _

⊕ **Coda**

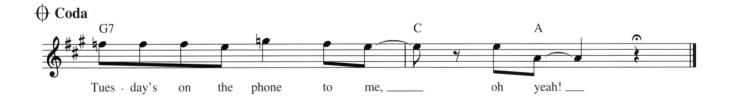

Tues-day's on the phone to me, _____ oh yeah! ___

Additional Lyrics

3. And so I quit the p'lice department,
    And got myself a steady job.
    And though she tried her best to help me,
    She could steal but she could not rob.

She Loves You

Words and Music by John Lennon and Paul McCartney

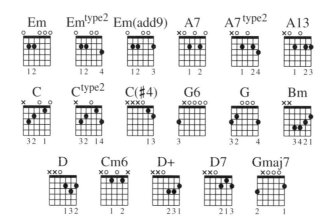

Strum Pattern: 2
Pick Pattern: 4

Intro-Chorus
Moderately

She loves you, yeah, yeah, yeah. _ She loves you, yeah, yeah, yeah. _ She

loves you, yeah, yeah, yeah, yeah. _____ 1. You think you've lost your love?

___ Well, I saw her yes-ter-day. ___ It's you she's think-ing of. ___ And she

told me what to say: ___ She says she loves you and you know that can't be ___ bad.

Yes, she loves you and you know you should be glad. _____ 2. She

Verse

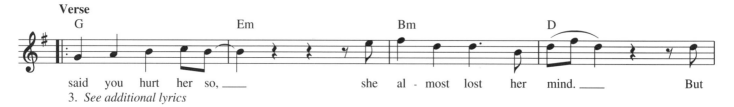

said you hurt her so, ___ she al-most lost her mind. ___ But

3. See additional lyrics

now she says she knows _ you're not the hurt - ing kind. _____ She says she

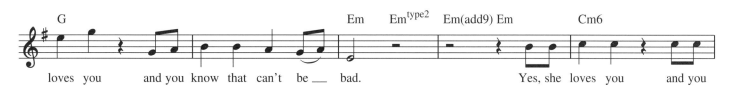

loves you and you know that can't be _ bad. Yes, she loves you and you

know you should be glad. _____ Oo! __ She loves you, yeah, yeah, yeah. _ She

loves you, yeah, yeah, yeah. _ And with a love like that you know you should be glad. _

_____ 3. You _____ With a love like that you

know you should be glad. _____ With a love like that you

know you should _____ be glad. Yeah, yeah, yeah. _ Yeah,

yeah, yeah. _ Yeah, yeah, yeah, yeah.

Additional Lyrics

3. You know it's up to you,
   I think it's only fair.
   Pride can hurt you too;
   Apologize to her.
   Because she loves you
   And you know that can't be bad.
   Yes, she loves you
   And you know you should be glad. Oo!

Something

Words and Music by George Harrison

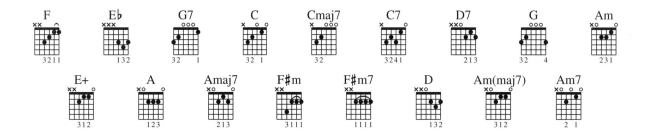

Strum Pattern: 3
Pick Pattern: 4

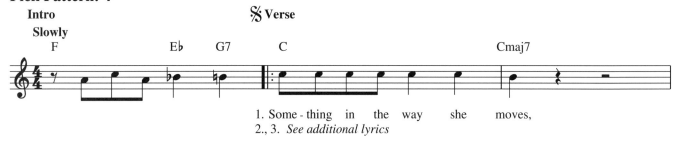

D   G   A   Amaj7

know _____ I don't know.   You stick a - round now, it may

F#m   F#m7   D   G   C

show,   I don't know _____ I don't know.

Guitar Solo

C   Cmaj7   C7

F   C   D7   G   Am   G

D.S. al Coda

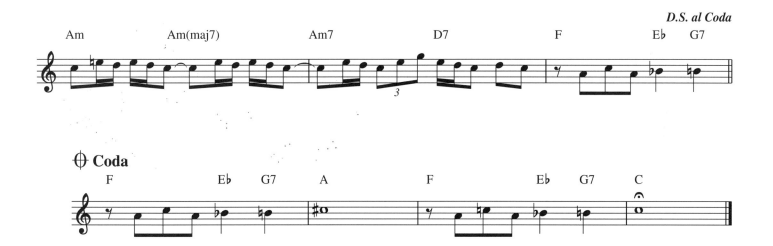

Am   Am(maj7)   Am7   D7   F   Eb   G7

⊕ Coda

F   Eb   G7   A   F   Eb   G7   C

Additional Lyrics

2. Somewhere in her smile she knows,
   That I don't need no other lover.
   Something in her style that shows me.
   I don't want to leave her now,
   You know I believe and how.

3. Something in the way she knows,
   And all I have to do is think of her.
   Something in the things she shows me.
   I don't want to leave her now,
   You know I believe and how.

Sun King

Words and Music by John Lennon and Paul McCartney

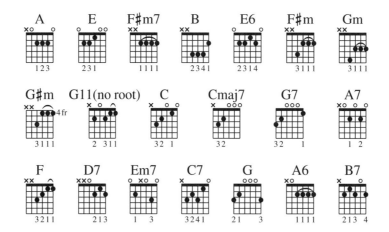

Strum Pattern: 3, 4
Pick Pattern: 1, 3

Slowly

Ah. _____ Here comes the

Sun King. Here comes the Sun King.

Ev - 'ry - bod - y's laugh - ing, _____ ev - 'ry - bod - y's hap - py. _____

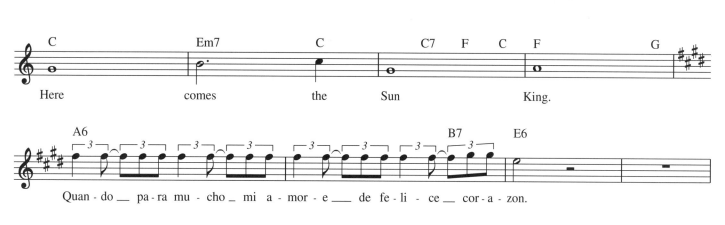

Here comes the Sun King.

Quan-do __ pa-ra mu-cho __ mi a-mor-e __ de fe-li-ce __ cor-a-zon.

Mun-do __ pa-pa-raz-zi __ mi a-mor-e __ chick-a fer-dy __ pa-ra sol.

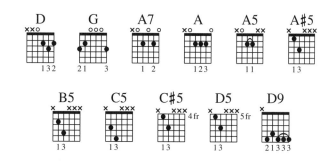

Cues-to __ ob-ri-ga-do tan-ta mu-cho __ que can eat it __ car-ou-sel.

Twist and Shout

Words and Music by Bert Russell and Phil Medley

Strum Pattern: 2
Pick Pattern: 4

Intro
Moderately

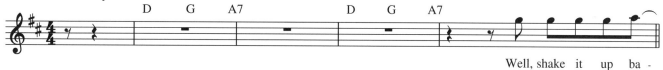

Well, shake it up ba-

-by, __ now. (Shake it up ba-by.) Twist and shout. __ (Twist and shout.) __

__ Come on, come on, __ come on, __ come on, ba-by, __ now. (Come on ba-

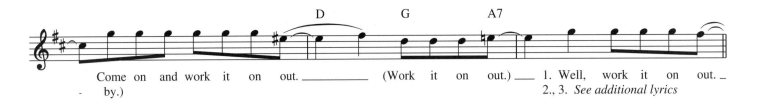

Come on and work it on out. _____ (Work it on out.) ___ 1. Well, work it on out. _
- by.)   2., 3. *See additional lyrics*

Verse

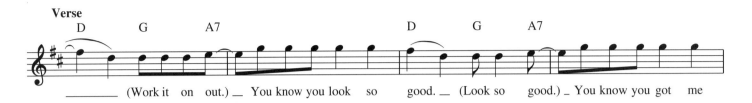

_____ (Work it on out.) _ You know you look so good. _ (Look so good.) _ You know you got me

go-in' now. (Got me goin'.) _ Just like I knew you would. _ (Like I knew you would.) _

1. | 2.   **Interlude**

___ Well, shake it up ba- ___   Ah.

Play 4 times

D.S. al Coda

Ah.   Ah.   Ah.   Ah. _____   Shake it up ba -

Coda   **Outro**

___ Well, shake it, shake it, shake it,   ba - by,   now. _   Well, shake it, shake it, shake it,
(Shake it up, ba - by.) ___

ba-by,   now. _   Ah.   Ah.   Ah.   Ah.
(Shake it up, ba - by.) _

Additional Lyrics

2., 3. You know you twist, little girl, (Twist little girl.)
        You know you twist so fine. (Twist so fine.)
        Come on and twist a little closer now. (Twist a little closer.)
        And let me know that you're mine. (Let me know you're mine.)

Ticket to Ride

Words and Music by John Lennon and Paul McCartney

Strum Pattern: 4
Pick Pattern: 1

1. I (3.) think I'm gon-na be sad. ___ I think it's to-day,
2., 4. *See additional lyrics*

___ yeah. ___ The girl that's driv-in' me mad ___ is go-in' a-way.

Chorus

She's got a tick-et to ride. ___

She's got a tick-et to ri - hi - hide. _ She's got a tick-et to ride, ___ but she don't care. _

4th time, To Coda

1. ___ 2., 4. She ___

2. **Bridge**

I don't know why she's rid-in' so high.

She ought-ta think twice, she ought-ta do right by me. Be -

fore she gets through say - in' good-bye, ___ she ought-ta think twice, she ought-ta do right by

D.S. al Coda
(take repeat)

Coda

Outro

Repeat and fade

me. 3. I ___ My ba-by don't care.

Additional Lyrics

2., 4. She said that livin' with me is bringin' her down, yeah.
For she would never be free when I was around.

Taxman

Words and Music by George Harrison

Strum Pattern: 2
Pick Pattern: 4

Verse
Moderate Rock

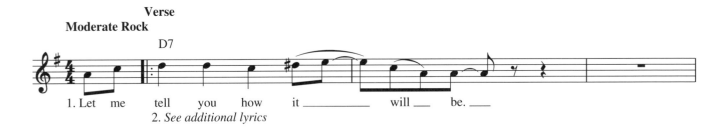

1. Let me tell you how it _____ will __ be. ___
2. *See additional lyrics*

There's one for you, nine - teen for __ me. ___

Chorus

'Cause I'm the tax - man, yeah, ___ I'm the tax - man. ___

2. Should five - If you drive a car, I'll

Bridge

tax the street. __ If you try to sit, I'll tax your __ seat. If your get too cold, I'll

tax the heat. __ If you take a walk, I'll __ tax your __ feet.

Chorus

Tax - man! _____ 'Cause I'm the tax - man. Yeah, ___ I'm the

Verse

tax - man. _____ 3. Don't ask me what I
4. *See additional lyrics*

want it for. ___ Ah, ah, _____ Mis - ter Wil - son. ___ If

you don't want to pay some more. __ Ah, ah, _____ Mis - ter Heath. _

Chorus

___ 'Cause I'm the tax - man. Yeah, ___ I'm the tax - man. ____

1. ___ 2. 4. Now my ___ and you're work - ing for

Outro   *Repeat and fade*

no one but ___ me. Tax - man! _____

Additional Lyrics

2. Should five percent appear too small,
   Be thankful I don't take it all.

4. Now my advice for those who die.
   Declare the pennies on your eyes.

Wait

Words and Music by John Lennon and Paul McCartney

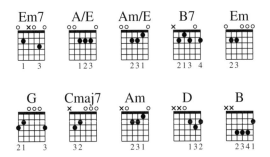

Strum Pattern: 6
Pick Pattern: 4

Intro
Moderate Rock

1. It's been a

Verse

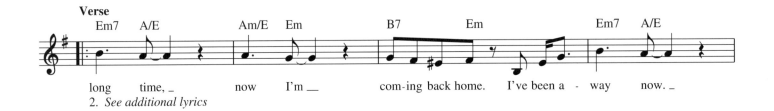

long time, _ now I'm _ com-ing back home. I've been a - way now. _
2. *See additional lyrics*

Oh, how _ I've been a - lone. _ Wait till I come back to your side, _

_ we'll for - get the tears we cried. _ 2. But if your _ I feel as

Bridge

though you ought to know that I've been good, as good as I can be. And if you

do,   I'll trust in you   and know that you   will wait for   me.   3. It's been a

4. *See additional*
                   lyrics

Verse

long   time, _   now I'm __   com-ing back home.   I've been a - way   now. _

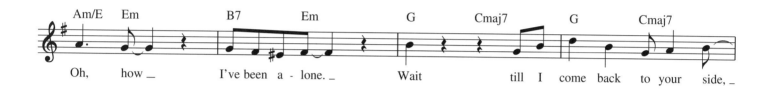

Oh,   how _   I've been a - lone. _   Wait   till I   come back   to your   side, _

——   we'll for - get   the tears we cried. _   I feel as ___   5. It's been a

Verse

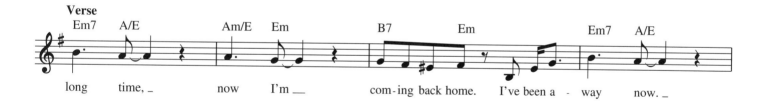

long   time, _   now I'm __   com-ing back home.   I've been a - way   now. _

Oh,   how ___   I've   been   a - lone.

Additional Lyrics

2., 4. But if your heart breaks,
        Don't wait, turn me away.
        And if your heart's strong,
        Hold on, I won't delay.
        Wait till I come back to your side,
        We'll forget the tears we cried.

We Can Work It Out

Words and Music by John Lennon and Paul McCartney

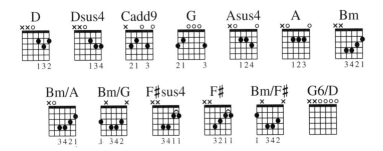

Strum Pattern: 2
Pick Pattern: 4

Verse
Moderately

1. Try to see it my way, do I have to keep on talk - ing
2. *See additional lyrics*

till I can't go on? While you see it your way, run a risk of know-ing that our

love may soon be gone. We can work it out, __ we can work it out. _____

Bridge

Life is ver - y short __ and there's no time _____ for fuss - ing and

fight - ing, my friend. I have al - ways thought __ that it's a crime. __

so I will ask you once a - gain.

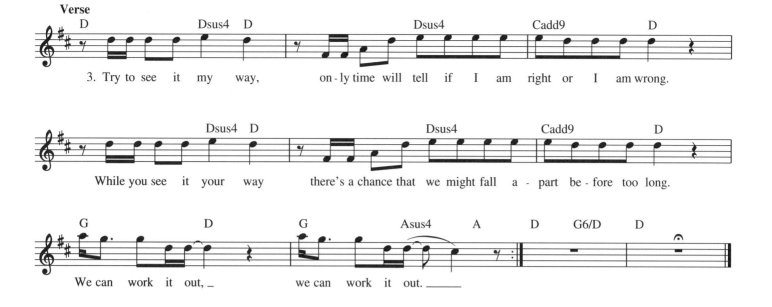

3. Try to see it my way, on-ly time will tell if I am right or I am wrong.

While you see it your way there's a chance that we might fall a - part be - fore too long.

We can work it out, _ we can work it out. _____

Additional Lyrics

2. Think of what you're saying,
   You can get it wrong and still you
   Think that it's alright.
   Think of what I'm saying,
   We can work it out and get it
   Straight, or say goodnight.
   We can work it out,
   We can work it out.

When I'm Sixty-Four

Words and Music by John Lennon and Paul McCartney

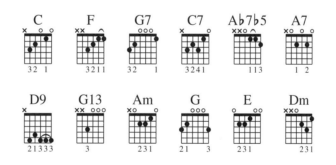

Strum Pattern: 2
Pick Pattern: 4

Intro
Moderately

Verse

1. When I get old - er, los - ing my hair _ man - y years from now, _

will you still be send-ing me a val-en - tine, _ birth-day greet-ings

bot-tle of wine? _ If I'd been out _ till quar-ter to three _ would you lock the door? _

Will you still need _ me, will you still feed _ me when I'm six-ty - four?

Bridge

Ooh. _ You'll be old - er

too. _ Ah. _ And if you say the word _

I could stay with you.

%̶ Verse

2. I could be hand - y mend-ing a fuse _ when your lights have gone. _
3. *See additional lyrics*

You can knit a sweat-er by the fire - side. _ Sun-day morn-ing go for a ride. _

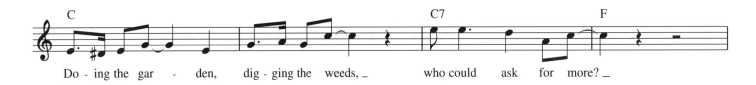

Do - ing the gar - den, dig - ging the weeds, _ who could ask for more? _

162

Will you still need _ me, will you still feed _ me, when I'm six-ty - four?

Bridge

Ev - 'ry sum - mer we can rent a cot - tage in the Isle of Wight _ if it's not too dear. _

_ We shall scrimp and save; _____

02

grand - chil - dren on your knee; ____ Ve - ra,

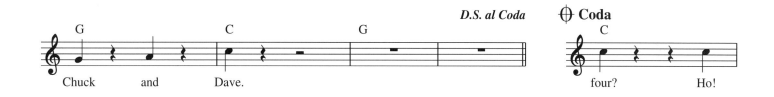

Chuck and Dave. four? Ho!

Additional Lyrics

3. Send me a postcard, drop me a line
Stating point of view.
Indicate precisely what you mean to say;
Yours sincerely, wasting away.
Give me your answer, fill in a form;
Mine forevermore.
Will you still need me,
Will you still feed me,
When I'm sixty-four?

While My Guitar Gently Weeps

Words and Music by George Harrison

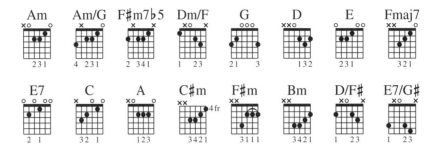

Strum Pattern: 2
Pick Pattern: 4

See additional lyrics

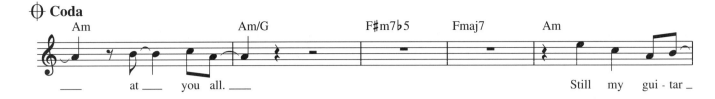

Coda

Am | Am/G | F#m7♭5 | Fmaj7 | Am |

_____ at _____ you all. _____ Still my gui-tar _____

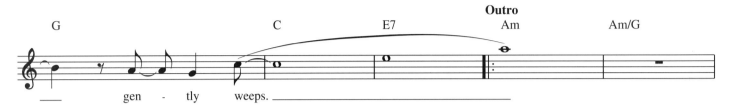

G | C | E7 | **Outro** Am | Am/G |

_____ gen - tly weeps. _____

Repeat and fade

F#m7♭5 | Fmaj7 | Am | Am/G | D | E7 |

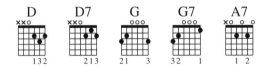

Additional Lyrics

Bridge I don't know why
You were diverted,
You were perverted, too.
I don't know how
You were inverted,
No one alerted you.

Why Don't We Do It in the Road

Words and Music by John Lennon and Paul McCartney

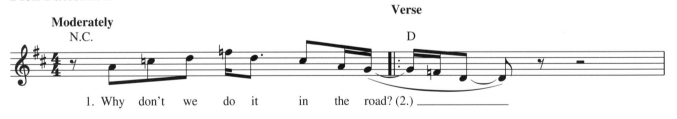

D   D7   G   G7   A7

Strum Pattern: 1
Pick Pattern: 2

Moderately
N.C.

Verse
D

1. Why don't we do it in the road? (2.) _____

D7

Why don't we do it in the road? _____   Why don't we do it in the road? _

Why don't we do it in the road? ____

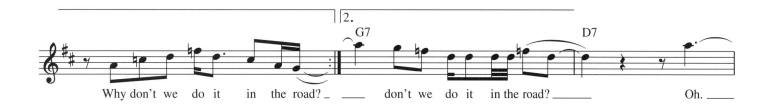

No one will be watch-ing us; ____ why ____ don't we do it in the road? ____

Why don't we do it in the road? ____ ____ don't we do it in the road? ____ Oh. ____

Verse

____ 3. Why ___ don't we do it ____ in the road? Why don't we do it in ___ the road? _

Why don't we do it, do ___ it in the road? ____

Why don't we do it in ___ the road? ____ No ___

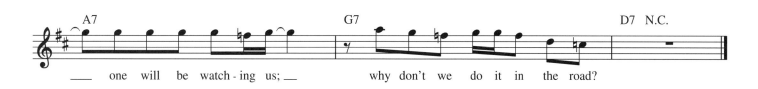

____ one will be watch-ing us; ___ why don't we do it in the road?

With a Little Help from My Friends

Words and Music by John Lennon and Paul McCartney

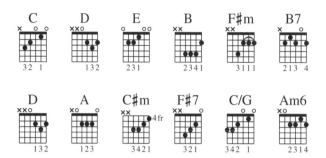

Strum Pattern: 4
Pick Pattern: 4

Intro

Bil - ly Shears.

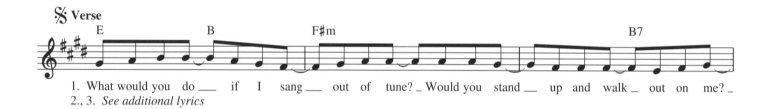

1. What would you do ___ if I sang ___ out of tune? __ Would you stand ___ up and walk __ out on me? __
2., 3. *See additional lyrics*

___ Lend me your ears ___ and I'll sing ___ you a song ___ and I'll try ___

___ not to sing ___ out of key. ___ {1., 3. Oh,}
                                    {2. No, } I get by ___ with a lit-tle help __ from my friends. __

___ Mm, I get high ___ with a lit-tle help __ from my friends. __ {1., 2. Mm,}
                                                                   {3. Oh, } I'm gon-na try __

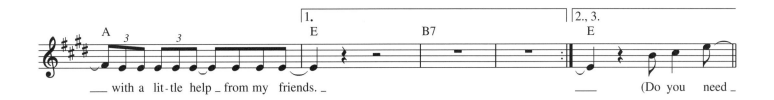

___ with a lit-tle help ___ from my friends. ___ (Do you need ___

Bridge

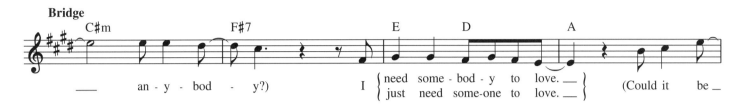

___ an-y-bod-y?) I { need some-bod-y to love. ___ }
{ just need some-one to love. ___ } (Could it be ___

To Coda ⊕

*D.S. al Coda
(take 2nd ending)*

___ an-y-bod-y?) I want some-bod-y to love. ___

⊕ **Coda**

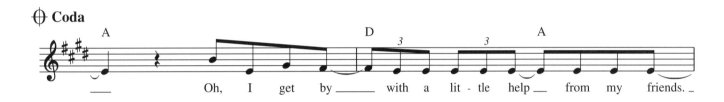

___ Oh, I get by ___ with a lit-tle help ___ from my friends. ___

___ Mm, I'm gon-na try ___ with a lit-tle help ___ from my friends. ___ Oh, I get high ___

___ with a lit-tle help ___ from my friends. ___ Yes, I get by ___ with a lit-tle help ___ from my friends, ___

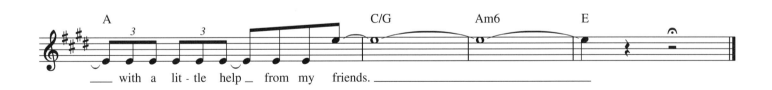

___ with a lit-tle help ___ from my friends. ___

Additional Lyrics

2. What do I do when my love is away?
   (Does it worry you to be alone?)
   How do I feel by the end of the day?
   (Are you sad because you're on your own?)

3. (Would you believe in a love at first sight?)
   Yes, I'm certain that it happens all the time.
   (What do you see when you turn out the light?)
   I can't tell you but I know it's mine.

Yellow Submarine

Words and Music by John Lennon and Paul McCartney

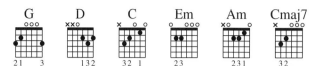

Strum Pattern: 2
Pick Pattern: 4

Verse
Moderately

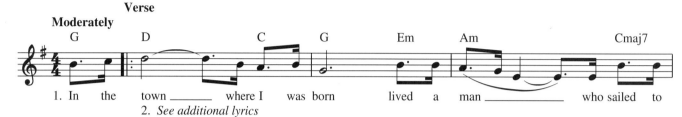

1. In the town _____ where I was born lived a man _____ who sailed to
2. *See additional lyrics*

sea. And he told _____ us of his life in the land _____ of sub - ma -

rines. 2. So we rine. We all live in a yel - low sub - ma-rine, yel - low sub - ma-rine,

yel - low sub - ma-rine. We all live in a yel - low sub - ma-rine, yel - low sub - ma-rine,

yel - low sub - ma-rine. 3. And our friends _____ are all on board, man - y more of them live next

door. And the band _____ be-gins to play:

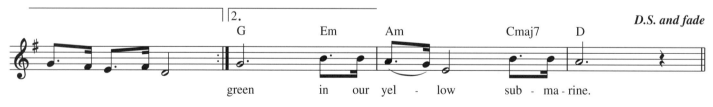

green in our yel - low sub - ma - rine.

Additional Lyrics

2. So we sailed up to the sun
   Till we found the sea of green.
   And we lived beneath the waves
   In our yellow submarine.

4. As we live a life of ease,
   Ev'ry one of us has all we need.
   Sky of blue and sea of green
   In our yellow submarine.

Yesterday

Words and Music by John Lennon and Paul McCartney

Strum Pattern: 1, 3
Pick Pattern: 2, 4

Additional Lyrics

2. Suddenly, I'm not half the man I used to be.
There's a shadow hanging over me.
Oh, yesterday came suddenly.

Yer Blues

Words and Music by John Lennon and Paul McCartney

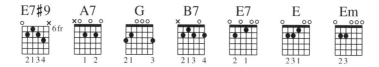

*Strum Pattern: 8

*Pick Pattern: 8

Intro
Slowly

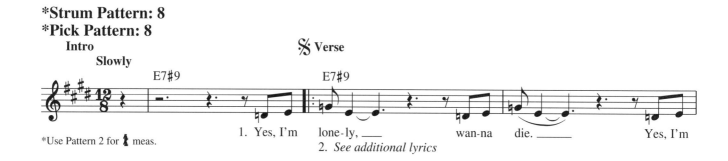

*Use Pattern 2 for ♩ meas.

1. Yes, I'm lone-ly, ___ wan-na die. ___ Yes, I'm
2. *See additional lyrics*

lone - ly, ___ wan - na die. ___ If I ain't dead al - read-y, ___

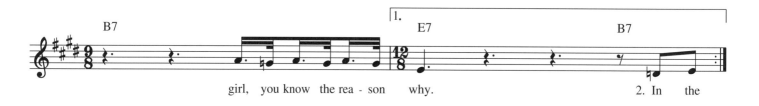

girl, you know the rea - son why. 2. In the

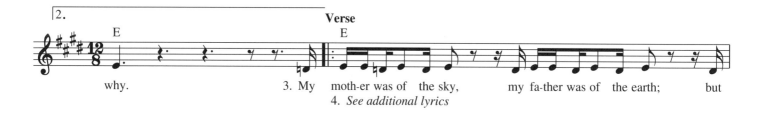

why. 3. My moth-er was of the sky, my fa-ther was of the earth; but
4. *See additional lyrics*

I am of the u - ni-verse, and you know what that's worth. ___ I'm lone - ly, ___ wan - na

die. ___ If I ain't dead al - read - y, ___

girl, you know the rea - son   why.   4. The

why.   5. The black   cloud crossed my mind,   blue mist round my soul.

Double-time feel

Feel   so   su - i - ci - dal,   e - ven   hate   my   rock and roll. _____ Wan-na   die, ___

yeah, _____   wan - na   die. ___   If   I

ain't   dead al - read - y,   girl,   you know   the rea - son why.

Outro

Repeat and fade

Additional Lyrics

2. In the mornin', wanna die;
   In the evenin', wanna die.
   If I ain't dead already,
   Girl, you know the reason why.

4. The eagle picks my eye, the worm, he licks my bones;
   I feel so suicidal, just like Dylan's Mister Jones.
   I'm lonely, wanna die.
   If I ain't dead already,
   Girl, you know the reason why.

You Never Give Me Your Money

Words and Music by John Lennon and Paul McCartney

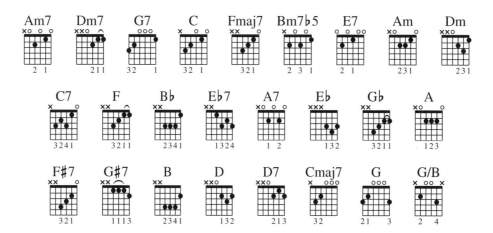

Strum Pattern: 1
Pick Pattern: 2

But oh, ___ that mag - ic feel - ing, no-where to go.

Oh, that mag - ic feel - ing, no - where to go, ___ no - where to go. ___

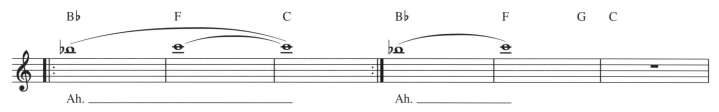

Ah. ___ Ah. ___

One sweet dream. ___ Pick up the bags and get in the lim - ou - sine. ___

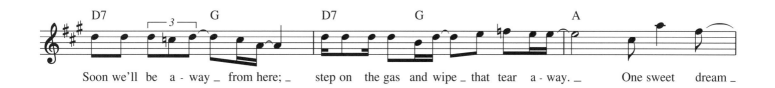

Soon we'll be a - way ___ from here; ___ step on the gas and wipe ___ that tear a - way. ___ One sweet dream ___

___ came true ___ to - day, ___ came true ___ to - day. ___

Repeat and fade

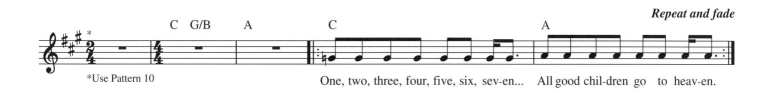

*Use Pattern 10

One, two, three, four, five, six, sev-en... All good chil-dren go to heav-en.

175

You've Got to Hide Your Love Away

Words and Music by John Lennon and Paul McCartney

Strum Pattern: 9
Pick Pattern: 7

1. Here I stand head in hand, turn my face to the wall.
2. *See additional lyrics*

If she's gone I can't go on feel-ing two foot small.

Ev-'ry-where peo-ple stare each and ev-'ry day. I can see them

laugh at me. And I hear them say:

"Hey, you've got to hide your love a-way! Hey, you've got to

hide your love a-way!"

Additional Lyrics

2. How can I even try, I can never win.
Hearing them, seeing them, in the state I'm in.
How could she say to me love will find a way?
Gather 'round all you clowns, let me hear you say: